WALKING THE
PYRENEES

Titles in the Footpaths of Europe Series

Normandy and the Seine
Walking through Brittany
Walks in Provence
Coastal Walks: Normandy and Brittany
Walking the Pyrenees
Walks in the Auvergne

WALKING THE
PYRENEES

Translated by Bob Hosea, Helen McPhail
and Suzanne Davies

Translation co-ordinator: Ros Schwartz

Robertson McCarta

The publishers thank the following people for their help with this book: Isabelle Daguin, Philippe Lambert, Vicky Hayward, Gianna Rossi, Tessa Hatts and Henrietta McCall.

First published in 1989 by

Robertson McCarta Limited
122 King's Cross.
London WC1X 9DS

in association with

Fédération Française de la Randonnée Pédestre
8 Avenue Marceau
75008 Paris

Managing Editor Jackie Jones
Series design by Prue Bucknell
Production by Grahame Griffiths
Typeset by The Robertson Group, Llandudno
Planning Map by Robertson Merlin

Printed and bound in Hong Kong

British Library Cataloguing in Publication Data

Walking in the Pyrenees. — (Footpaths of Europe).
   1. France. Pyrenees. Visitors' guides
   I. Hosea, Bob II. McPhail, Helen III.
   Davies, Susan IV. Series
   796.5'22'094652

   ISBN 1 — 85365-165-6

CONTENTS

A note from the publisher

The books in this French Walking Guide series are produced in association and with the help of the Fédération Française de la Randonnée Pédestre (French ramblers' association) — generally known as the FFRP.

The FFRP is a federal organisation and is made up of regional, local and many other associations and bodies that form its constituent parts. Individual membership is through these various local organisations. The FFRP therefore acts as an umbrella organisation overseeing the waymarking of footpaths, training and the publishing of the Topoguides, detailed guides to the Grande Randonnée footpaths.

There are at present about 170 Topoguides in print, compiled and written by local members of the FFRP, who are responsible for waymarking the walks — so they are well researched and accurate.

We have translated the main itinerary descriptions, amalgamating and adapting several Topoguides to create new regional guides. We have retained the basic Topoguide structure, indicating length and times of walks, and the Institut Géographique National (official French survey) maps overlaid with the routes.

The information contained in this guide is the latest available at the time of going to print. However, as publishers we are aware that this kind of information is continually changing and we are anxious to enhance and improve the guides as much as possible. We encourage you to send us suggestions, criticisms and those little bits of information you may wish to share with your fellow walkers. Our address is: RobertsonMcCarta, 122 King's Cross Road, London WC1X 9DS.

We shall be happy to offer a free copy of any one of these books to any reader whose suggestions are subsequently incorporated into a new edition.

It is possible to create a variety of routes by referring to the walks above and to the planning map (inside the front cover). Transport and accommodation are listed in the alphabetical index in the back of the book.

KEY

Gournay

This example shows that you can expect the walk from Gournay to Arbois to take 2 hours, 10 minutes.

2:10

ARBOIS
⌂ Å ✗ ⚒ ▭
14th century church

Arbois has a variety of facilities, including hotels and buses. Hotel addresses and bus/train connections may be listed in the index at the back of the book.

a grey arrow indicates an alternative route that leaves and returns to the main route.

Detour

indicates a short detour off the route to a town with facilities or to an interesting sight.

Symbols:

⌂ hotel;
⌂ youth hostel, hut or refuge;
Å camping;
✗ restaurant;
♆ cafe;

⚒ shops;
━ railway station;
▭ buses;
⛴ ferry;
🅑 tourist information

THE FOOTPATHS OF FRANCE

by Robin Neillands

W hy should you go walking in France? Well, walking is fun and as for France, Danton summed up the attractions of that country with one telling phrase: 'Every man has two countries,' he said, 'his own . . . and France.' That is certainly true in my case and I therefore consider it both a pleasure and an honour to write this general introduction to these footpath guides to France. A pleasure because walking in or through France is my favourite pastime, an honour because these excellent English language guides follow in the course set by those Topo-guides published in French by the Fédération Française pour la Randonnée Pédestre, which set a benchmark for quality that all footpath guides might follow. Besides, I believe that good things should be shared and walking in France is one of the most pleasant activities I know.

I have been walking in France for over thirty years. I began by rambling — or rather ambling — through the foothills of the Pyrenees, crossing over into Spain past the old Hospice de France, coming back over the Somport Pass in a howling blizzard, which may account for the fact that I totally missed two sets of frontier guards on both occasions. Since then I have walked in many parts of France and even from one end of it to the other, from the Channel to the Camargue, and I hope to go on walking there for many years to come.

The attractions of France are legion, but there is no finer way to see and enjoy them than on foot. France has two coasts, at least three mountain ranges — the Alps, Pyrenees and the Massif Central — an agreeable climate, a great sense of space, good food, fine wines and, believe it or not, a friendly and hospitable people. If you don't believe me, go there on foot and see for yourself. Walking in France will appeal to every kind of walker, from the day rambler to the backpacker, because above all, and in the nicest possible way, the walking in France is well organised, but those Francophiles who already know France well will find it even more pleasurable if they explore their favourite country on foot.

The GR system

The Grande Randonnée (GR) footpath network now consists of more than 40,000 kilometres (25,000 miles) of long-distance footpath, stretching into every part of France, forming a great central sweep around Paris, probing deeply into the Alps, the Pyrenees, and the volcanic cones of the Massif Central. This network, the finest system of footpaths in Europe, is the creation of that marvellously named organisation, *la Fédération Française de Randonnée Pédestre, Comité National des Sentiers de Grande Randonnée,* which I shall abbreviate to FFRP-CNSGR. Founded in 1948, and declaring that, *'un jour de marche, huit jours de santé* the FFRP-CNSGR has flourished for four decades and put up the now familiar red-and -white waymarks in every corner of the country. Some of these footpaths are classic walks, like the famous GR65, *Le Chemin de St. Jacques,* the ancient Pilgrim Road to Compostela, the TMB, the *Tour du Mont Blanc,* which circles the mountain through France, Switzerland and Italy, or the 600-mile long GR3, the *Sentier de la Loire,* which runs from the Ardèche to the Atlantic, to give three examples from the hundred or so GR trails available. In addition there is an abundance of GR du Pays or regional footpaths, like the *Sentier de la Haute Auvergne,* and the *Sentier Tour des Monts d'Aubrac.* A 'Tour' incidentally, is usually a circular walk. Many of these regional or provincial GR trails are charted and waymarked in red-and-yellow by local outdoor organisations such as ABRI (Association Bretonne des Relais et Itineraires) for Brittany, or CHAMINA for the Massif Central. The walker in France will soon become familiar with all these footpath networks, national, regional or local, and find them the perfect way into the heart and heartland of France. As a little bonus, the GR networks are expanding all the time, with the detours — or *varientes* — off the main route eventually linking with other GR paths or *varientes* and becoming GR trails in their own right.

Walkers will find the GR trails generally well marked and easy to follow, and they have two advantages over the footpaths commonly encountered in the UK. First, since they are laid out by local people, they are based on intricate local knowledge of the local sights. If there is a fine view, a mighty castle or a pretty village on your footpath route, your footpath through France will surely lead you to it. Secondly, all French footpaths are usually well provided with a wide range of comfortable country accommodation, and you will discover that the local people, even the farmers, are well used to walkers and greet them with a smile, a *'Bonjour'* and a *'bonne route'*.

Terrain and Climate
As a glance at these guides or any Topo-guide will indicate. France has a great variety of terrain. France is twice the size of the UK and many natural features are also on a larger scale. There are three main ranges of mountains, the Alps contain the highest mountain in Europe, the Pyrenees go up to 10,000 ft, the Massif Central peaks to over 6000 ft, and there are many similar ranges with hills which overtop our highest British peak, Ben Nevis. On the other hand, the Auvergne and the Jura have marvellous open ridge walking, the Cévennes are steep and rugged, the Ardeche and parts of Provence are hot and wild, the Île de France, Normandy, Brittany and much of Western France is green and pleasant, not given to extremes. There is walking in France for every kind of walker, but given such a choice the wise walker will consider the complications of terrain and weather before setting out, and go suitably equipped.

France enjoys three types of climate: continental, oceanic, and mediterranean. South of the Loire it will certainly be hot to very hot from mid-April to late September. Snow can fall on the mountains above 4000 ft from mid-October and last until May, or even lie year-round on the tops and in couloirs; in the high hills an ice-axe is never a frill. I have used one by the Brêche de Roland in the Pyrenees in mid-June.

Wise walkers should study weather maps and forecasts carefully in the week before they leave for France, but can generally expect good waether from May to October, and a wide variety of weather — the severity depending on the terrain — from mid-October to late Spring.

Accommodation
The walker in France can choose from a wide variety of accommodation with the asurance that the walker will always be welcome. This can range from country hotels to wild mountain pitches, but to stay in comfort, many walkers will travel light and overnight in the comfortable hotels of the *Logis de France* network.

Logis de France: The *Logis de France* is a nationwide network of small, family-run country hotels, offering comfortable accommodation and excellent food. *Logis* hotels are graded and can vary from a simple, one-star establishment, with showers and linoleum, to a four- or five-star *logis* with with gastronomic menus and deep pile-carpets. All offer excellent value for money, and since there are over 5000 scattered across the French countryside, they provide a good focus for a walking day. An annual guide to the *Logis* is available from the French Government Tourist Office, 178 Piccadilly, London W1V 0AL, Tel (01) 491 7622.

Gîtes d'Etape: A *gîte d'etape* is best imagined as an unmanned youth hostel for outdoor folk of all ages. They lie along the footpath networks and are usually signposted or listed in the guides. They can be very comfortable, with bunk beds, showers, a well equipped kitchen, and in some cases they have a warden, a *guardien*, who may offer meals. *Gîtes de étape* are designed exclusively for walkers, climbers, cyclists, cross country skiers or horse-riders. A typical price (1989) would be Fr.25 for one night. *Gîtes de étape* should not be confused with a *Gîte de France*. A *gîte* — usually signposted as *'Gite de France'* — is a country cottage available for a holiday let, though here too, the owner may be more than willing to rent it out as overnight accommodation.

Youth hostels: Curiously enough, there are very few Youth Hostels in France outside the main towns. A full list of the 200 or so available can be obtained from the Youth Hostel Association (YHA), Trevelyan House, St. Albans, Herts AL1 2DY.

Pensions or cafes: In the absence of an hotel, a *gîte d'etape* or a youth hostel, all is not lost. France has plenty of accommodation and an enquiry at the village cafe or bar will usually produce a room. The cafe/hotel may have rooms or suggest a nearby pension or a *chambre d'hôte*. Prices start at around Fr.50 for a room, rising to say, Fr.120. (1989 estimate).

Chambres d'hôte: A *chambre d'hôte* is a guest room, or, in English terms, a bed-and-breakfast, usually in a private house. Prices range from about Fr.60 a night. *Chambres d'hôte* signs are now proliferating in the small villages of France and especially if you can speak a little French are an excellent way to meet the local people. Prices (1989) are from, say, Fr.70 for a room, not per person.

Abris: Abris, shelters or mountain huts can be found in the mountain regions, where they are often run by the *Club Alpin Francais,* an association for climbers. They range from the comfortable to the primitive, are often crowded and are sometimes reserved for members. Details from the Club Alpin Francais, 7 Rue la Boétie, Paris 75008, France.

Camping: French camp sites are graded from one to five star, but are generally very good at every level, although the facilities naturally vary from one cold tap to shops, bars and heated pools. Walkers should not be deterred by the *'Complet'* (Full) sign on the gate or office window: a walker's small tent will usually fit in somewhere. *Camping à la ferme,* or farm camping, is increasingly popular, more primitive — or less regimented — than the official sites, but widely available and perfectly adequate. Wild camping is officially not permitted in National Parks, but unofficially if you are over 1500m away from a road, one hour's walk from a *gîte* or campsite, and where possible ask permission, you should have no trouble. French country people will always assist the walker to find a pitch.

The law for walkers
The country people of France seem a good deal less concerned about their 'rights' than the average English farmer or landowner. I have never been ordered off land in France or greeted with anything other than friendliness . . . maybe I've been lucky. As a rule, walkers in France are free to roam over all open paths and tracks. No

decent walker will leave gates open, trample crops or break down walls, and taking fruit from gardens or orchards is simply stealing. In some parts of France there are local laws about taking chestnuts, mushrooms (and snails), because these are cash crops. Signs like *Réserve de Chasse*, or *Chasse Privé* indicate that the shooting is reserved for the landowner. As a general rule, behave sensibly and you will be tolerated everywhere, even on private land.

The country code

Walkers in France should obey the *Code du Randonneur.*

- Love and respect nature.
- Avoid unnecessary noise.
- Destroy nothing.
- Do not leave litter.
- Do not pick flowers or plants.
- Do not disturb wildlife.
- Re-close all gates.
- Protect and preserve the habitat.
- No smoking or fires in the forests. (This rule is essential and is actively enforced by foresters and police).
- Respect and understand the country way of life and the country people.
- Think of others as you think of yourself.

Transport

Transportation to and within France is generally excellent. There are no less than nine Channel ports: Dunkirk, Calais, Boulogne, Dieppe, Le Havre, Caen/Ouistreham, Cherbourg, Saint-Malo and Roscoff, and a surprising number of airports served by direct flights from the UK. Although some of the services are seasonal, it is often possible to fly direct to Toulouse, Poitiers, Nantes, Perpignan, Montpellier, indeed to many provincial cities, as well as Paris and such obvious destinations as Lyon and Nice. Within France the national railway, the SNCF, still retains a nationwide network. Information, tickets and a map can be obtained from the SNCF. France also has a good country bus service and the *gare routière* is often placed just beside the railway station. Be aware though, that many French bus services only operate within the *département,* and they do not generally operate from one provincial city to the next. I cannot encourage people to hitch-hike, which is both illegal and risky, but walkers might consider a taxi for their luggage. Almost every French village has a taxi driver who will happily transport your rucksacks to the next night-stop, fifteen to twenty miles away, for Fr.50 a head or even less.

Money

Walking in France is cheap, but banks are not common in the smaller villages, so carry a certain amount of French money and the rest in traveller's cheques or Eurocheques, which are accepted everywhere.

Clothing and equipment

The amount of clothing and equipment you will need depends on the terrain, the length of the walk, the time of your visit, the accommodation used. Outside the mountain areas it is not necessary to take the full range of camping or backpacking gear. I once walked across France from the Channel to the Camargue along the Grande Randonneé footpaths in March, April and early May and never needed to use any of the camping gear I carried in my rucksack because I found hotels everywhere, even in quite small villages.

Essential items are:
In summer: light boots, a hat, shorts, suncream, lip salve, mosquito repellent, sunglasses, a sweater, a windproof cagoule, a small first-aid kit, a walking stick.
In winter: a change of clothing, stormproof outer garments, gaiters, hat, lip salve, a companion.
In the mountains at any time: large-scale maps (1:25,000), a compass, an ice-axe. In winter, add a companion and ten-point crampons.
At any time: a phrase book, suitable maps, a dictionary, a sense of humour.

The best guide to what to take lies in the likely weather and the terrain. France tends to be informal, so there is no need to carry a jacket or something smart for the evenings. I swear by Rohan clothing, which is light, smart and fuctional. The three things I would never go without are light, well-broken-in boots and several pairs of loop-stitched socks, and my walking stick.

Health hazards:
Health hazards are few. France can be hot in summer, so take a full water-bottle and refill at every opportunity. A small first-aid kit is sensible, with plasters and 'mole-skin' for blisters, but since prevention is better than the cure, loop-stitched socks and flexible boots are better. Any French chemist — a *pharmacie* — is obliged to render first-aid treatment for a small fee. These pharmacies can be found in most villages and large towns and are marked by a green cross.

Dogs are both a nuisance and a hazard. All walkers in France should carry a walking stick to fend off aggressive curs. Rabies — *la rage* — is endemic and any-one bitten must seek immediate medical advice. France also possesses two types of viper, which are common in the hill areas of the south. In fairness, although I found my walking stick indispensable, I must add that in thirty years I have never even seen a snake or a rabid dog. In case of real difficulty, dial 17 for the police and the ambulance.

Food and wine
One of the great advantages with walking in France is that you can end the day with a good meal and not gain an ounce. French country cooking is generally excellent and good value for money, with the price of a four-course menu starting at about Fr.45. The ingredients for the mid-day picnic can be purchased from the village shops and these also sell wine. Camping-Gaz cylinders and cartridges are widely available, as is 2-star petrol for stoves. Avoid naked fires.

Preparation
The secret of a good walk lies in making adequate preparations before you set out. It pays to be fit enough to do the daily distance at the start. Much of the necessary information is contained in this guide, but if you need more, look in guidebooks or outdoor magazines, or ask friends.

The French
I cannot close this introduction without saying a few words about the French, not least because the walker in France is going to meet rather more French people than, say, a motorist will, and may even meet French people who have never met a foreigner before. It does help if the visitor speaks a little French, even if only to say *'bonjour'* and *'Merci'* and *'S'il vous plait'*. The French tend to be formal so it pays to

be polite, to say 'hello', to shake hands. I am well aware that relations between France and England have not always been cordial over the last six hundred years or so, but I have never met with hostility of any kind in thirty years of walking through France. Indeed, I have always found that if the visitor is prepared to meet the French halfway, they will come more than halfway to greet him or her in return, and are both friendly and hospitable to the passing stranger.

As a final tip, try smiling. Even in France, or especially in France, a smile and a *'pouvez vous m'aider?'* (Can you help me?) will work wonders. That's my last bit of advice, and all I need do now is wish you *'Bonne Route'* and good walking in France.

WALKING THE PYRENEES

by Kev Reynolds

The GR10 *Sentier des Pyrénées* is one of the great walks of France; a European classic with all the ingredients required to create an experience of lasting memory for anyone who tackles it - either as a whole, or in isolated sections.

And what are those ingredients?

First must come scenic grandeur, for there are few regions I know that can match the Pyrénées for landscape variety. There are green moulded hills, savage aiguilles, glacier-carved valleys, dazzling snowfields, meadows rich with the most extravagent flora in Europe, broad swollen rivers, dancing mountain torrents, lakes and forests and deep limestone gorges.

There are villages of undisputed Gallic charm, like Lescun on its belvedere of pasture below Pic d'Anie, or Laruns in a bowl of mountain greenery. Or such villages as Ainhoa nestling in the Basque country where art and architecture are one and the same. Or at the opposite end of the range, in that sun-trap of a valley, the Cerdagne, there's the old fortressed township of Mont-Louis on the edge of the high granite desert of the Carlit massif.

And, of course, there's the scale of the walk to take into account.

Some 400 kilometres separate the Atlantic and the Mediterranean; four hundred kilometres of magnificent landscapes. But not even a Pyrénéan crow would fly from one to the other in a straight line, and the GR10 nearly doubles that distance on its journey east from Hendaye to Banyuls. 700-odd kilometres of footpath, track and country lane will take the fit mountain walker anything from five to seven weeks to complete. And there are optional loops, too, and tempting diversions to tease the single-minded wanderer into side valleys or over cols that beckon with the promise of more fine views.

The GR10 is at once a challenge and a temptation, but it should be stressed that it is not the sole preserve of the hardened long-distance walker, for there are countless individual outings that would fill the odd day of a touring holiday with quiet pleasure, and give to the more general tourist the sort of insight into the mountain world that is normally only to be experienced by the adventurous trekker, while for those who would devote a fortnight's holiday to a long walk, it lends itself to a convenient breakdown into three of four different sections. The GR10 leads gently to a flavour of true wilderness whilst never straying far from human dimensions.

Unlike the High Route (*Haute Randonnée Pyrénéenne*), under normal summer conditions the GR10 involves no specialised mountaineering skills or equipment. Whilst the High Route strays often into Spain, GR10 remains entirely on French territory and finds convenient, if sometimes strenuous, passages over the intervening ridges. Neither is it necessary to treat the walk as a backpacking expedition, for there are *gîtes d'étape*, mountain huts (*refuges*) and villages with assorted overnight accommodation liberally spread along the length of this route, and regular opportunities to restock with provisions for those who prefer to cook their own meals - which will be necessary in some unmanned refuges.

However, to walk in France is also to indulge in one of the favourite pastimes of the French; that of eating. Anyone who plans to tackle the GR10 will be denying themselves one of the pleasures of the region if they steadfastly insist on providing their own meals throughout. All over France the produce of kitchen and wine cellar alike have attained the heights of gastronomic artistry, and regional specialities of Pyrénéan cuisine include the duck cutlet of Bigorre, *canard magret,* a Basque omelette, *Jambon Piperade,* and assorted cheeses. Trout are plentiful in the mountain streams and will often feature in various guises on restaurant menus. (There is a particular back-of-beyond *hôtellerie* I know, hidden in a little valley just off the route of the GR10, where the proprietor spends most of his days thigh-deep in a clear but icy torrent angling for the dinner table of his guests. Occasions have been known when a climbing friend and I have made five-hour diversions from our planned itinerary simply to sit at the table of this unassuming, yet richly satisfying hotel, and to feast on the *patron's* sport!) The Pyrénées have other such surprises and rewards in store, and walking along the GR10 will provide plenty of opportunities to sample them.

The route officially begins beside the Atlantic at Hendaye on the right bank of the Bidassoa which forms the Franco-Spanish border. This is Basque country: a region of green wooded hills and lush valleys watered by the mild Atlantic mists and rain to form a rampant vegetation. Gorse and bracken clothe the hillsides while attractive villages, farms and isolated houses occupy well considered positions from which the hills are laid out in all their splendour. Shepherds take their flocks into the mists and trails wind everywhere to confuse. Happily the GR10 is waymarked with care.

Near Pic d'Anie, which marks the end of Basque lands and the beginning of the so-called High Pyrénées, there's an extensive area of limestone pavement that produces a remarkable contrast to the wooded country to the west. Then comes Lescun, whose pastoral setting is as idyllic as one could possibly wish. Guarding the village are the twin Pics Billare, and to the south a veritable forest of limestone peaks jostling one against another and forming the Spanish frontier. Here would be a fine place to stay awhile and to explore neighbouring valleys in an orgy of discovery.

Beyond the deep, glacier-scoured Aspe Valley, you come under the spell of Pic du Midi d'Ossau, known to all as Jean-Pierre; perhaps the most distinctive of all Pyrénéan mountains. And again one is tempted to delay departure by making the classic Tour of Pic du Midi, a one- or two-day circuit of the peak. Or, better still, the longer and more demanding Tour de la Haute Vallée d'Ossau which will require four or five days of walking. Indeed, it would not be difficult to find sufficient outings to warrant a fortnight's holiday in this area alone.

Having made a long diversion north to avoid the granite wilderness of the Balaitous massif, a GR10 *variante* heading south through the Gaube Valley is worth taking for the spectacular views it presents of the North Face of the Vignemale (3,298 metres), highest summit on the international frontier. From there to Gavarnie is one of the classic day's walking in these mountains, crossing as it does the lofty Hourquette d'Ossoue and descending below the retreating icefield of the Ossoue Glacier, while the Cirque de Gavarnie itself rightfully occupies a place high on the list of every visitor to the Pyrénées.

For some distance the GR10 traverses in and out of sections of the National Park, and the eastern-most limits of this Park are to be found in the Néouvielle massif, a delight of sparkling tarns and shapely peaks; a real mecca for the lover of untarnished mountain scenery. This is yet another region worth taking time properly to explore.

Bagnères de Luchon sits about midway across the range. Immediately to the east the Spanish border has forced northward in order to enclose the Val d'Aran, one of those geographical anomalies of which the Pyrénées have so many. GR10 then works a route round the boundary too, in wooded country with sweeping hillsides of grass dashed by fast-flowing streams, and skirts the fine peak and imposing ridges of Mont Valier (2,838 metres), climbed first in 1672.

Haute Arriège, between *Luchonnais* and the Carlit massif, has some of the wildest and least-known mountains of the range, with deep valleys cut between important, yet little-trod projecting ridges. The route here avoids all major difficulties, though, while still maintaining a lively interest to Mérens-les-Vals on the Ax-Andorra road.

The crossing of the Carlit massif is a delight, with its extensive lakes and scattered tarns lying like pearl necklaces round the gaunt granite peaks. Yet again this is an area that would repay a detailed study, and a glance at the map will inspire a bounty of daydreams to turn into reality. But the eastern heights, washed with Mediterranean clarity, draw the wanderer on. Catalonia can be unbearably hot in midsummer, but the sun-washed hills and orchard-clad valleys at last give way to the gentle lapping of the sea. There you can dispense with walking boots and rucksack and submerge yourself in the refreshing calm of the Mediterranean.

Henry Russell, the romantic Franco-Irish mountaineer who was the greatest publicist the Pyrénées ever knew, wrote wisely a hundred years ago: 'The Alps astound, the Pyrénées attract and soften us...The Mountains have an Oriental grace and langour...It is to the Pyrénées that the smiles of the artist and the heart of the poet will always turn'.

To that I would add: so too will the dreams of the walker. But beware; the Pyrénées can be habit-forming.

WALK 1

HENDAYE
⌂ △ ⚓ ✗ ⛽
🚂 ℹ️

Seaside resort renowned for its bathing; several, marked, long distance walks.

1:10

RN10

1:0

BIRIATOU
⌂ △ ✗

(see map ref A)
50m
Basque church

The GR10, like the `*Haute Randonnée Pyrénéenne*' begins at Hendaye-Plage by the casino. Start opposite the casino and walk along Boulevard Général Leclerc. Passing a public garden on the right, follow Rue des Citronniers, then take the boulevard to the left along the Baie de Chingoudy; 50 metres before a bridge go down Rue de Belcenia on your left. Taking Rue Parcheteguia, turn left along Rue de Subornea. Cross the railway via the subway and go up the lane immediately ahead which comes out on a road. Follow it for 60 metres before branching eastwards on an uphill stretch of tarmac which leads to a gravel path. This soon widens to allow access to a villa at the top of the small hill. The path branches left, to the south-east, passes under two electric cables, becomes overgrown, climbs a small hill and then drops down towards the RN10.

Follow the road uphill to the left; 50 metres further on take a steep turn to the right above a brick hut. The path is rather overgrown with bushes and passes over a crest before plunging steeply towards a tarmac road. You go up the road, following it to the right, after passing a house called Chabaldegui. When you come to a minor tarmac road, turn left and continue for some 50-100 yards before turning right towards the motorway. Use a cattle track to pass beneath it. Ahead of you is the right side of a small valley; follow it, taking a path which rises slightly and then drops down, first to a farm and then to a stream, which you cross. A steep rise brings you to a narrow tarmac lane leading down south-eastwards to Maison Mouniort overlooking Biriatou. Only those wishing to break the journey here go down to Biriatou.

Biriatou can also be reached by car on the D258. From the village centre, walk up a tarred lane and then a stony path heading eastwards up a small ridge with electricity pylons. You take a winding and overgrown path between the first two pylons to the right

© IGN carte N° 1245

(south-east), leaving the rocky ledges of the Choldokagagna due left. This path leads right up to the Col d'Osin (374 metres). Go down a grassy path in a south-easterly direction. Initially it has very few markings. Follow it as far as the Col des Poiriers (Pear Tree Pass, 316 metres), which dominates the north-eastern edge of the lake bearing the same name. Climb again in a south-easterly direction along the edge of a larch plantation until you reach the Col des Joncs. (Rush Pass, 384 metres). Keep on walking uphill and south-eastwards. Just before you come to a stream, follow the horizontal path to the left. This leads to a grassy spur, which takes you gently uphill towards the south-east to join a path forming a balcony on the north flank of the Mandale. Walk eastwards along it. Above a conifer plantation you will come to a wide path leading down to a long series of *ventas* or old Spanish wayside inns.

COL D'IBARDIN

(see map ref B)
317m

Take the D404 for 50 metres or so, heading north, until you join a path on the right which leads upwards, first to the north-east and then eastwards. You go over the crest (380 metres) and down into the valley (north-east) taking the path on the left bank. When you come to the bottom of an old sandstone quarry, follow its stony access road to the north-west. Where the road levels out, 100 metres before the D404, go straight down into the wooded valley, heading east, until you come to a path on the left bank, which becomes gradually more distinct. Before you reach IGN map ref 115L, take a wide path going south towards a stream. Walk upstream on the western bank as far as frontier marker 18. You enter Spain at this point. Continue for another 400 metres as far as Venta d'Inzola.

VENTA D'INZOLA

115m

Pick up the path 20 metres to the north and cross the concrete footbridge. Now climb up the path ahead, going through the gate and then veering right in a south-easterly direction, then a short while later to the left. You leave Spain, and climb out of a wooded valley on its left bank to reach the Col du Grand-Escargas (274 metres).

From here, follow a good path on the edge of the slope heading northwards and leading to the hamlet of Olhette.

OLHETTE

⌂ ✕

65m

1:30

Col des Trois Fontaines

(see map ref C)

563m

Detour

⌂

300m to the north.

0:20

La Rhune Railway Station

543m

1:15

The GR10 follows the right bank of the swiftly flowing Larroungo southward. After a while, it heads diagonally south-east, and then loops round (257 metres). Take a path which runs alongside the 'Miramar' rocks and leads to the Col des Trois Fontaines.

Keep following the path eastwards, leaving a marshy area to your left, and later a boggy dip in the land to your right. Make sure you follow the red and white markers carefully to avoid going down to the village of Ascain on your left. Cross a stream to the right of a low wall forming a small dam, and walk up again for a few metres until you reach a small grove of conifers to the east.

From this ledge, you cross the tracks and go down (south-eastwards) into the valley on a path which runs along its left side. Initially, the path also runs parallel to the railway line, which is directly above. In 15 minutes you reach a sheepfold, overlooking a huge enclosure, which you skirt round to the left. At an altitude of about 240 metres you leave the track, which bears right, to take a path, on the left or eastward side, which drops a little, levels out and then, runs along a meadow on the right, rising slightly to go over a spur. It continues downward to the edge of a wood, where you come to a restored farm at the end of a stony path. Leaving the farm on the right, go down the path. You pass in front of a residential farmhouse with an enormous water cistern (140 metres high). Some 90 metres further down you come to a farm with a breeze-block barn, where you take a more rustic path, crossing a stream and climbing up to another farmhouse restored in 1976. Leave the path and go down to the right, avoiding the farm on your left on the uphill side by taking a muddy track which runs round a small valley and then leads up towards Aldumieda Farm. Using the farm's stony track, continue downhill. You come out on a small tarmac road. Turn left and follow it to Sare.

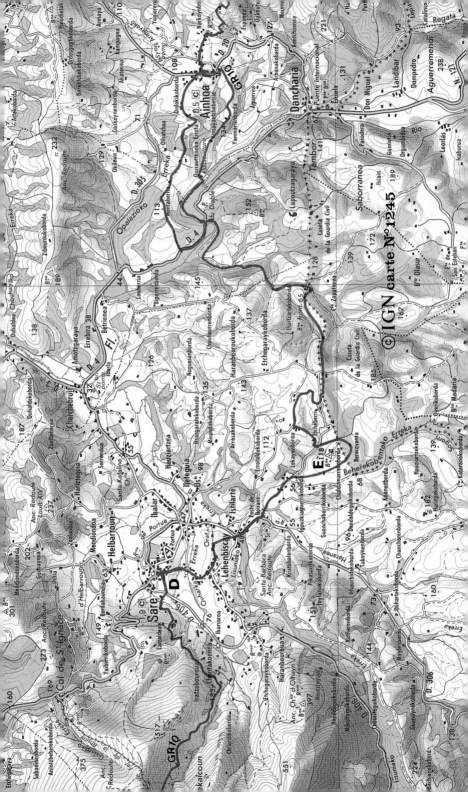

© IGN carte N° 1245

SARE

(see map ref D)
70m;
Typical basque village.
Three marked walks of 3-5
hours.

1:0

VENTA BEROUET

(see map ref E)
100m

The frontier, running regardless of the topography and encroaching significantly on the northern slopes, forces walkers to leave the mountains for a few hours between Sare and Ainhoa. These two picturesque villages are, of course, connected by 8.5 kilometres of departmental roads.

From the centre of Sare at the parking area by the front wall of the pelota court, retrace your steps along a road which runs south-south-west. After 10 metres, on a bend, turn off and go down a cul de sac, which continues as a grassy path lined with flagstones. Cross a stream on large sandstone flagstones.

Leaving a chapel to the right and a road to the left, cross a bridge and follow a tarmac path to within sight of a second chapel. Leave this on the left and go up a path behind it to the south-west as far as marker 86, where you join a tarmac path in Lehenbiscay. Take this path to the left, pass one road on the right. After Mendachainea house, the path becomes a dirt track. Continue along this, heading eastwards. Leave a ruined house to your left, and take a muddy path on the right (south) leading to the road from Sare-Col to Lizarrieta. Follow it southwards. You come to a crossroads (48 metres) and see an old bridge on the left. After 300 metres, leave the road for the pass and the customs post on your right, and carry straight on in the direction of the frontier inns. You come to a small bridge and then pass a farm to the left; 200 metres further on turn off the tarmac on to a dirt track on the right. Leaving a farm to the right, walk up to and go round the height mark 118 to emerge in the huge car park at Venta Berouet.

Leave the Venta on the right. The GR loops round to the north to avoid some private property. Walk 200 metres down the road towards Sare, then take the right fork towards La Venta Urt-Txola for 100 metres until you reach a path on the left (north). This leads to a small road heading right to Ledayenborda Farm. From there, follow the La Venta Galza Gorri road, first in an easterly and then a south-easterly direction. When you reach a copse, leave the road and follow a path to the left which runs along a fence and comes out opposite La Venta.

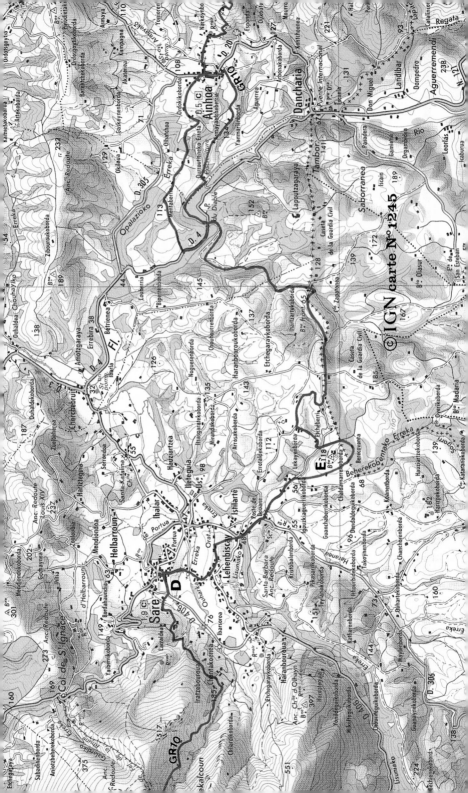

© IGN carte Nº 1245

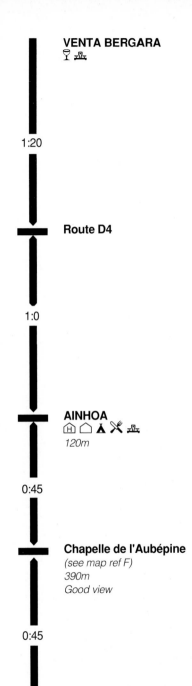

VENTA BERGARA

1:20

Route D4

1:0

AINHOA
120m

0:45

Chapelle de l'Aubépine
(see map ref F)
390m
Good view

0:45

Leave it to the right and take a small road heading eastwards along the frontier. You come to 63 and the Venta Bergara (see left). Continue eastwards. Level at first, the path first descends, passing a Spanish farm on the right, and rises again. At marker stone 65, take the path on the right going down to an inn which is closed. You leave the frontier at this point, on a path heading north-north-east. At a bridge, leave the road temporarily and follow the right bank of the stream. After a short while, return to the road, which joins the D4 road at Pont du Diable (the Devil's Bridge).

Do not cross the bridge. Walk up along the wooded bank of the Nivelle via the picnic area. You will see an old mill to the left on the far bank. When you come to the bridge belonging to the fish farm, cross it and then leave the fish farm to your right. Take a path heading southwards and overlooking the Nivelle. Five minutes later it goes down to an old track. Turn left onto this (east). Continue, following a stream, going up into a wood, crossing two fences, and coming out on a road which, after 1 kilometre, leads to the south of the village of Ainhoa.

From the square by the pelota wall, take the D20 southwards. When you reach the cemetery surrounding the church, take a small road to the left (east). Pass a chapel to your right and, further on, the hotel Argi-Eder to your left. The lane climbs towards a watertank and a water trough; at the crossroads take steep Stations of the Crosspath to the Chapelle de l'Aubépine (Hawthorn Chapel).

Leave the chapel, heading in a north-easterly direction on a grassy track which passes directly behind the three crucifixes. The track rises gently and continues as an almost horizontal path through a hollow depression on the west flank of the Ereby. The track then passes over the north-west spur of the mountain at an altitude of 413 metres. Bear south-east, and climb up a gentle rise to a pass (490 metres), where there is a drinking trough and drinking water. This pass, on the north-east of the Ereby, can also be reached via a track which comes up from Espelette. Follow this track southwards along the east flank of the

Ereby to reach the Col des Trois Croix (Three Crosses Pass).

Col des Trois Croix
510m

Important: Except in bad weather leave the route circling the Atchoulegui by its southern flank.

Climb eastwards for several minutes towards the east on the crest. Take a wide and not very clear grass path, which encircles the Atchoulegui on its north flank at an average altitude of 500 metres. Twenty minutes later you rejoin the road and follow it down (south-east) as far as a pass (430 metres), the meeting place of many trails and paths. Leaving a black boarded wooden hunters' hut on the left, keep straight on; the path rises a bit, descends along the ridge to a small pass, and then goes up again, leaving a small white house with a sheepfold on the right. Still climbing upwards, bear left, cross several streams in a valley bottom, and continue up as far as the Col Zuccuta.

1:0

Col Zuccuta
566m
Not marked on the IGN
1/50,000 map, the pass
lies to the south-west of the
Ourrezti Peak.
(see IGN map ref 566)

Alternative route from Col Zuccuta to Esteben Farm. On a good day you can walk along the top of the ridge (south-south-west) with good views in every direction. After 45 minutes you come to frontier marker 76, some 100 metres before the Col de Gorospil, which is in Spain. From there plunge straight down north-eastwards to join the GR at Esteben Farm.

Continue southwards. Do not go up the ridge named Mont Bizkayluze, but instead take the cliff path on the eastern side as far as Esteben Farm.

1:0

ESTEBEN FARM
⌂ ♈ ⚏
(see map ref G)
580m

Cross the farmyard, making sure that you close the gate, and follow a wide path to the Col dex Veaux (Calves' Pass, 540 metres).

COL DEX VEAUX
⌂
(3 minutes southwards).
Detour
⚔
To the north the track
rejoins the road down to
Laxia. Walk down this for
2.5km

1:0

Go round a paddock to the left and, above, below the ridge forming the frontier. Follow a path north-eastwards to join the tarmac road, which climbs up to the Artzamendi radar installations. Follow it for 1 kilometre as far as Col de Méhatche.

Col de Méhatche
Frontier marker 80.

Follow a path eastwards that starts on the flat but soon bears diagonally a little to the right, passing a standing stone at frontier markers 82 and 83. Go through a paving stone works and descend a little before continuing on the flat in a southeasterly direction. 100 metres before the Cithabourou sheepfold (640 metres) which you leave to your left, go carefully down into the ravine, first going south-west, and then, before reaching the bottom, bear left and eastwards to join a path in the scree at the foot of the rocks. This corniche path goes round a spur. After that ignore all the footpaths on the right.

You pass below the grotto of the Saint-qui-sue (the Sweating Saint), which is partly hidden (see map ref H).

The path goes down towards a farm with a tiled roof. Skirt the fence and take the road to Bidarray but at the second bend follow the old footpath which is a shortcut. Then rejoin the road for 2 kilometres.

2:30

You will reach a bridge on the Bastan; cross it and 50 metres before you reach the second bridge (le Pont du Diable or the Devil's Bridge), take a winding footpath which climbs up to the right until you come to a path on a ledge; follow it to the left (east) to the village of Bidarray.

BIDARRAY
⌂
150 metres
Rescue service/first aid.
The village centre with the church, the pelota court and the town hall is on a small hill.

Leave by a small street to the East in the Noblia area on the D978 and the Nive. The itinerary continues over the Crêtes d'Iparla - one of the great classic Basque routes. Under the eye of the vultures you overlook magnificent sheer precipices and, if the sky is clear, you have a view of more than 100 kilometres from the Atlantic to the Pic d'Anie.

NOBLIA area
🏠 🚉 🚍

1:15

From the Noblia area go up again, up the small road; pass by the church and the pelota court and continue on the same road westwards, bearing left where it does. You go right where the road forks and go up on the second path to the right leading to the Ordaburia farm, turn left and continue between tall chestnut trees. This path climbs to the peaks of Iparla which are reached at the Col avec une Bergerie.

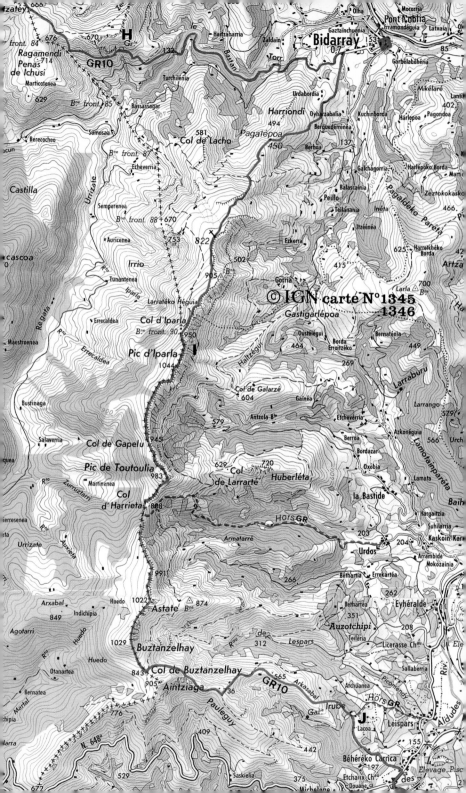

Col avec une Bergerie
(Sheepfold Pass)
450m
Named Pagalepoa on the
IGN 1.25,000 map.

1:45

Pic d'Iparla
(see map ref I)
1,044m

1:0

Col d'Harrieta
808m. A cool, wooded
spot, ideal for a rest.
Detour. *1 hr 30 min.*
URDOS.

The GR continues upward to the left (south-west) on a well-marked path. You pass a derelict sheepfold to the left of the path on the edge of the precipice. A little further on the paths fork.

Alternative route from fork to IGN map ref 822. The next stretch of the GR is very mountainous; the non-mountaineering walker can branch off diagonally to the right on a good mule track, marked in blue, passing the north flank of the mountain, and continuing as far as a sheep with an enclosure, called Bourouzune Koborda. From here, walk up to the left (south-east) and rejoin the GR near a stone cross, which is slightly below IGN map ref 822, on the edge of the cliffs.

Follow the route to the left on a rough, but well-marked ridge path, along the eastern side of the mountain, which loops round a rocky peak. You reach the ruins of a sheepfold (727 metres), and a large standing stone; then walk up to a grassy pass (770 metres). From here, continue southwards along the ridge. This is just the edge of a grassy plateau, which slopes slightly towards the west, but to the east rises in magnificent peaks, which you look down upon for several hours. You pass the Larra Téko-Héguia (962 metres), and follow the ridge which drops slightly to Col d'Iparla, only to rise again towards milestone 90 on, the frontier, which comes down diagonally from the north irrespective of the terrain. Continue along the route to the Iparla Peak.

Heading in a south-westerly direction, follow footpaths slightly to the right of the crest, which rises to two more 'peaks' of some 1,042 and 1,017 metres before dropping down to the Col de Gapelu (945 metres). Continue southwards, leaving the Toutoulia Peak (939 metres) to your left. Go down into the hollow to the south-west at Col d'Harrieta.

Detour, see left. Follow a path going down to the north-east. After 700 metres leave the path and the ridge and descend to the right (south) along the edge of a meadow. There is

a large sheepfold at the bottom which can be used to provide shelter (630 metres). Continue down, heading south, passing another meadow to your left and coming to a hut (560 metres). From here, head south-eastwards along a path, which drops down into a valley bottom. Cross a stream 430 metres further on and take the right bank eastwards. Then you cross a road leading to the village of Urdos. From here it is 4 kilometres by road to Saint-Etienne-de-Baïgorry.

1:45

Leaving a horizontal path to the west, go up the ridge into the forest. This steep climb takes you to the Astaté (1,022 metres). Continue along the crest, which goes down a small gorge (960 metres) and then climbs to Buztanzelhay Peak (1,028 metres), the last of the high points on this section. Then climb down a rocky and fairly steep slope to Col de Buztanzelhay. You can make this an easier descent by veering right to follow natural ridges in the rock or sheep tracks.

Col de Buztanzelhay
843m

Head down the valley on the left (east) to join a clearly defined path on the right bank near a large tree. This is the last spring between here and Saint-Etienne-de-Baïgorry. The path descends down to the 700 metre level and then climbs again to the right along the hillside, reaching the crest to the east of Aintziaga Peak, at about 750 metres. Go down a little to the right of the crest as far as a kind of small pass (700 metres). Now leave the crest for an adjoining chain of mountains, and descend towards the left (north-east), passing two sheepfolds to your left. The path, cut out of the rocks, runs along the crest, slopes off a bit on the southern side, and rejoins the crest at a grassy pass. Continue along the crest following the grass path. Then, when you come to a bush, leave the ridge and take a path heading downhill to the left in a north-easterly direction. When you reach a wooden hut, take another path heading east, which is bounded on the left by a small wall. At a place called Irube you come to a road. Follow this down to the right (south), leaving a stony track to your right.

2:15

Detour
LEISPARS
⌂
(see map ref J).

Detour, see left. Follow the marked detour to the left on a wide, downhill path heading east-south-east. This cuts a loop out of the GR, then rejoins it for several metres eastwards. You then leave the GR again on a bend and head left on a sunken path (east) to Leispars. The GR10 continues along the road for about 200 metres. When it begins bearing north-eastwards, take a wide path through the forest for some 100 metres. Cross a gate and a stream on your left and then follow the footpath on the left bank. This brings you to the entrance of the park belonging to the Chateau d'Etchaux. Take the lane between the gateway and the pelota court at Baïgorry.

SAINT-ETIENNE-DE BAIGORRY
⌂ ⌂ Å ✕ ⚓
🚌 🛈

162m. Market town of Basse Navarre; Irouleguy vineyard.

Starting from the police station, follow a lane, heading east, for 300 metres. Go under a railway line and turn right on to a small road. Leave this on the second bend to climb up to the right on a gravel track along the edge of a wood.

Leave to your right a fork in the road and a house and continue in the same direction for another five minutes. You come out at the foot of a grass and bracken mound. Leaving a level path to the left (east), continue for about 10 metres and then climb the mound on a badly marked track which heads uphill to the left towards the south-east. Pass a sheepfold to the right, and then follow an almost horizontal path between two hedges. Skirt a second sheepfold to the left. When you come to the base of a hillock, follow the second path up to the right. After 100 metres, fork left and head for the top of the hillock. Part of the Oylarandoy range is clearly visible to the south. The summit is crowned with a clump of oak trees (450 metres). After a ledge, you join a path going diagonally to the left (east) towards a large tree on the edge of the old track between Saint-Etienne-de Baigorry and the Aharza Pass.

1:15

The old track to the
Col d'Aharza
(see map ref K)
521m

Continue to the right until you reach a crossroads (570 metres).

Alternative route from the crossroads to Col d'Aharza. The GR should be taken in bad weather, otherwise follow the crest to the top of the Oylarandoy (993 metres) and the chapel. There are fine views over the dock at Baïgorry

1:0

© IGN carte N°1346

and the low walls of the Iparla. From here you can make a direct, but somewhat steep, descent towards the Col d'Aharza.

Follow the GR west round the Oylarandoy until you reach Col d'Aharza.

Col d'Alharza
734m

Here you again meet the road heading towards the Col d'Urdanzia. However, unless the weather is good, ignore it in favour of the tracks along the ridge. From the pass, follow the road for about 100 metres and then climb up to the right, passing a sheepfold to the right. The path rises south-eastwards over bracken and undergrowth along the eastern flank of the Munhogain. Climb over the low wall of a field. Several metres to the left is the Leizarze Pass (828 metres). Continue climbing southwards for a few minutes; the path heads gradually leftwards, first to the south-east then east. Keeping the crest to the right, follow the path, which at first is almost horizontal but then descends to the Col d'Urdanzia.

Col d'Urdanzia
(see map ref L)
869m,
Iron Cross.
(760 metres)
400 metres north of the
pass, but well below it
a sheepfold offers possible
shelter. Take a path
leading off road

Alternative route from Col d'Urdanzia to Deux Abreuvoirs. If the weather is misty or changeable, take the new road which goes directly from the Col d'Urdanzia to the `Deux Abreuvoirs' (the two drinking troughs) via the eastern face of the Monhoa.

Turn left (north) off the alternative route at the 820metre point and follow the same road down to Lasse or Arnéguy.

Continue north-eastwards along the top of the ridge, beside a barbed wire enclosure, heading towards the Monhoa (1,021metres). On a fine day there is a magnificent view from here. Descend via the eastern ridge, passing some precipices and barbed wire on the left. Passing a mass of rocks at Béharria (870 metres) continue towards the east until you come to Deux Abreuvoirs.

Deux Abreuvoirs
750m

Here you leave the eastern ridge of the Monhoa and head off left on the north flank, following a path which descends to the north-west. Passing a watering place half way down the slope on the left, you come to an oak grove (570 metres). Strike off to the left (westwards) to find a path below a small sheepfold, going down towards the north-east along a small ridge. This brings you to the top of an east-facing slope. The path

©IGN carte N°1346

1:30

curves eastwards and then continues northwards. After 400 metres you come across several trees and a barbed wire enclosure. Bear right (east) and after 50 metres, join a path made by a bulldozer. Go down this to the left (north) after closing a gate. Down below, on the right, you can see a farm and a shepherd's hut. After 340 metres you reach a crossroads. On the left, in the woods, is a shepherd's hut. Bear right (east) and, shortly afterwards, bear left (towards the north), going round the back of the barbed wire enclosure belonging to the farm mentioned above. The path is now completely free of vegetation. It keeps to the east side of the hill (348 metres) and is replaced by a small tarmac road leading to the church as Lasse.

LASSE
⌂ ♉

(see map ref M)

0:30 *204m*

Follow the tarmac road eastwards towards Saint-Jean-Pied-de-Port. After 1 kilometre it climbs the Nive d'Arnéhuy and then, after another kilometre, it comes to Saint-Jean-Pied-de-Port.

SAINT-JEAN-PIED-DE-PORT
🏛 ⌂ ⚑ ✕ ⛴
🚌 🚃 ℹ

157m.
The former capital of Basse-Navarre, this picturesque stronghold is situated on both sides of the River Nive. 15th century town walls; 17th century fort; old houses and bridge; 18th century church; birthplace of Charles Floquet; son-et-lumière on summer evenings; junction with GR65.

0:50

In front of the church, turn your back on the bridge over the Nive and the Rue d'Espagne, and walk up the Rue de la Citadelle, which is lined with 17th and 18th century houses, for 300 metres. After the Porte Saint-Jacques, follow the path of that name which heads east. Pass a road on the right which climbs towards the south. Continue straight on as far as the crossroads (194 metres), where you take the D401 for 1 kilometre in the direction of Çaro. At a factory, which used to manufacture tiles, but now makes breeze-blocks (230 metres), go right along the driveway to an estate. Just in front of the gates, take a path to the left which heads south. This forks after a gate. Go left again, towards the north-east, on a path that is often muddy, but which runs into two tarmac tracks descending south-south-east to the D401 at the entrace to Çaro.

Çaro
(see map ref N)
246m

Basque pelota court; cemeteries with 17th and 18th century Navarrian tombs; 17th century stone

At the exit to the village, a crossroads points in the direction of Saint-Michel and D'Aincille: you take a tarmac path between the two and head south-east. At the foot of the grassy mound (IGN map ref 305), turn right on to a tarmac path, which encircles a small hill to the south. The path continues due south. You skirt a refuse tip, then cross a stream. Climb

© IGN carte N° 1346

crucifix; restored church with reredos and 18th century gallery.

1:45

towards the south-south-west, then westwards until, after a bend to the left, you reach the Ahadoa Farm (218 metres). Follow its access road southwards. At the first fork continue southwards on a small road straight ahead of you. A minute later, leave the tarmac road for a path but continue to head south. You cross a shooting range, and rejoin the path, which goes over a small pass at 410 metres. Follow the route along the north flank of the Handiamendi Crest. After a gate, you pass the ruins of a building, following a grassy path which runs below the ridge (east-south-east) to the Col d'Handiague.

Col d'Handiague
(see map ref O)
587m

1:30

Skirt the meadow in the pass to the right, passing through two gates. You then join a road suitable for motor vehicles and continue to the right (south-east). The road borders a farm (run on a share-cropping system), crosses the bottom of a valley with two small streams and climbs a grassy crest (583 metres) to the Emaga Farms. It then heads to the right (south-west), before veering westward, and zigzagging down along a spur to Estérençuby in the valley.

ESTERENÇUBY
🏠 ⌂ 🍴 ⛲
231m. Church with 18th century Basque-style gallery.

1:15

From the Mairie (Town Hall) climb the steep tarmac path heading south-east towards the church. Pass this to your left and go south up a wide path. Next follow a small tarred road south-east, passing first the entrance to the Harguinaénéa Farm on the left and then the Phagalcette road on the right. Keep going straight on (south-east) on another small road which overlooks Estérenguibel. About an hour after setting out from Estérencuby you come to a crossroads; keep going on an untarred road, heading first south-west and then south to the crest where, at a sort of pass, you find the Route de la Phagalcette.

Route de la Phagalcette
(see map ref P)
585m

1:0

Take the road heading south-east. After 40 metres the road forks: take the left-hand branch. After 400 metres, at an altitude of 640 metres, the GR leaves the tarmac road, which goes down to the left, and transfers to a wide path heading south-south-east. Continue in this direction crossing over four successive crossroads. You then skirt a wide circular meadow to the right and follow a track leading to a pass on the top of the Ithurramburu.

© IGN carte N°1346-1446

Pass on the top of the Ithurramburu
820m

1:45

The ridge-top path goes off to the right towards the Arthé Pass in the south-west. The GR descends to the south on a meadow track until you come to a bridge (653 metres) where the track climbs slightly north-eastwards again. Where it bears right, level with a sheepfold and a large beech tree, turn right on to an old footpath to climb a mountain spur, which at first is completely barren.

At an altitude of about 800 metres, the footpath leaves the crest and the trees to the left, enters a rocky gully and continues into the forest. The path traverses conglomerate rock, keeping to the south-west flank of the mountain. You emerge, at about 920 metres, into grassland. Climb up to a pass on the south-west of the Pic d'Irau, where you find the Route de Béhérobie in the Iraty Forest.

Route de Béhérobie in the Iraty Forest
1,025m

Follow this road for 800 metres westwards as far as the Col d'Irau (see map ref Q) at an altitude of 1,008 metres.

Detour, *45 min.*
◠

Take a country lane heading south.

2:30

Shortly afterwards, where paths coming from the south-west join the road, leave it to climb up in the open, with no path to follow, towards the south-east, passing Artaquieta wood due left. At an altitude of 1,250 metres you come across a rather faint jeep track heading towards the Pic d'Occabé (Occabé Peak). Walk round the cromlechs and, finally, leave the rocky debris from the top of the Occabé to your right. The track bears left (east) and descends, first in the open and then winding along the beech grove. You come out on a small tarmac road. Turn left and follow northwards until you reach the Chalet Pedro.

CHALET PEDRO
◠ ✕

(see map ref R)
990m

2:0

Continue north along the road for 1 kilometre as far as the artificial lake. Leave the road coming in from Béhérobie to your left and go right towards Col Bagarguiac. After a few hundred metres take the old jeep track on the right (north-east), which climbs up through the Iraty forest. It goes over a small pass (1,190 metres), and descends eastwards, widened and rutted by lumbering activity. You rejoin the Col Bagarguiac road, level with an artificial lake. Cross the road and the retaining wall and then turn right (east) on to a path that climbs in zigzags on to the crest

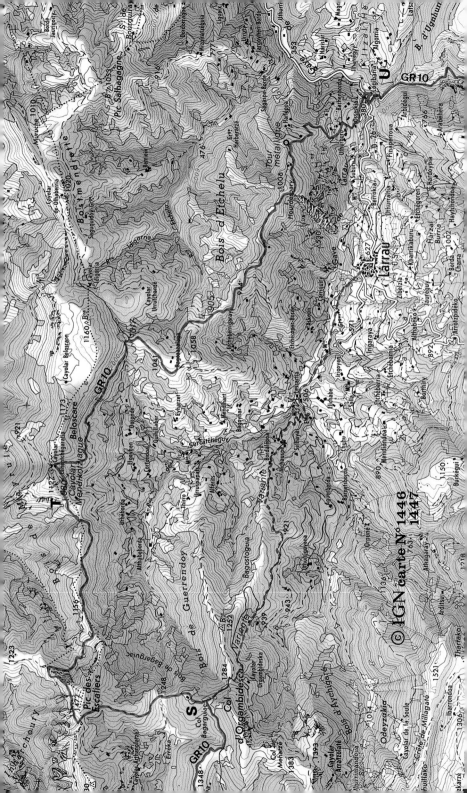

© IGN carte N°1446
1447

COL EGUICHOURI

COL BAGARGUIAC
(see map ref S)
1,327m

2:50

LARRAU
627m

Col Bagarguiac
(Bagarguiac Pass)

of the Eguichouria. Here it runs almost horizontally along the top towards the south-east, before bearing right (south) and going down to the Col Eguichouri at 1,319 metres (see left). Take the road heading east which, after 700 metres, reaches the Col Bagarguiac.

Alternative route from the Col Bagarguiac to Larrau, 2 hr 50 min. The former route of the GR10, this should be followed if the weather is bad. It is a less attractive, but quicker route. Follow the Larrau Road to the east. After 10 minutes you come to the Col d-Orgambidesca (1,284 metres). Traverse this, passing a series of hairpin bends to your right. After five minutes you cross these bends to reach an old track running below the Larrau Road. About 30 minutes after leaving the pass, cross the road again. After another 10 minutes, rejoin the road and walk downhill for 200 metres. Pick up the track again on your left as it goes up a small col, then narrows and descends. After 1 hour you come to the Forges de Larrau Road again (506 metres). Follow the road to the left in a south-easterly direction until it begins to rise again. This 10 minute walk brings you to a track leading to barns belonging to the Syndicat de Soule. Take a path passing between two barns for 50 metres and then cross a meadow, remembering to close the gates. This 20 minute stretch brings you to a big fork. Go right on a path that rises fairly steeply, levels off and then continues uphill. Another rise brings you out on the edge of a plateau. After 50 metres, pass a house on your right and, 50 metres further on, this 30 minute section of the walk takes you to the village of Larrau (see left).

Starting below the tennis courts, take a foresters' path, which descends first towards the north, then threads its way north-west. At the Col Iratzabaleta (1,248 metres) climb up again towards the north-east, then northwards on a footpath along the ridge. After a horizontal stretch (1,390 metres) it edges to the left a little, and climbs along the side of the pass to attack the Pic des Escaliers (the Staircase

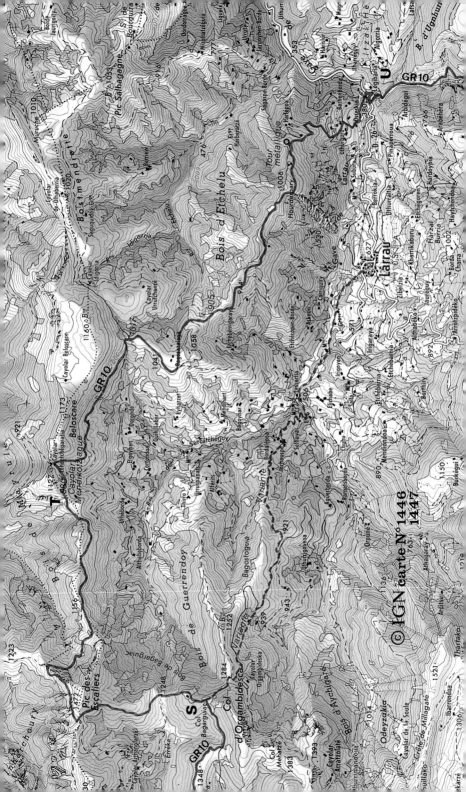

© IGN carte N° 1446
1447

2:10

Peak) from the west. Go over the crest at 1,423 metres, to the west of the Pic des Escaliers, which you will virtually encircle. Start walking north-eastwards on the spectacular Staircase Path which, at 1,280 metres, reaches the north-east spur of the peak. Walk down this spur to a road (1,250 metres). Follow it on the level as far as the Ugatzé Crest, to the south-east of the Pic des Escaliers.

Alternative route from Col de Bagarguiac to the Ugatzé Crest, 40 min. Follow the recently opened road link between the Col de Bagarguiac and Ahuzk until it crosses the GR10 on the Crest of the Ugatzé. This route saves you 1 hr 20 mins, but misses the superb Balcon des Escaliers (Balcony Staircase).

Crête Ugatzé
(not marked on the IGN map)
1,170m

0:40

Leave the road to follow the crest eastwards. It drops at first to the Col Ugatzé (1,145 metres). Next, you come to two unremarkable, rounded hilltops, which you pass in turn. At the pass (1,070 metres), with a chalet below on the right, follow a footpath going diagonally down to the south-east and bypassing the distance marker 1,107 to the south. You rejoin the crest at the pass (1,020 metres). Follow a track to the right that, after a few minutes, brings you to Cayolar Mendikotziague (Shepherd's Stone Shelter).

Cayolar Mendikotziague
(see map ref T)
980m

1:0

Leave the track and go down towards a drinking fountain, which is probably the only water you will find all day. Continue along the flank of the pass on horizontal and well-marked footpaths. Then take a better quality path, which heads down to the south-south-east. The footpath passes 20 metres to the left of a tumbledown shepherd's shelter (962 metres) and, after walking for another three minutes on the level beside a row of trees, take a gently rising footpath to the left. Climb over a rocky pass (975 metres), where you will find a dovecote, and continue south-eastwards, on quite a clear path, which runs along the south-west wide of the Beloscare Crest. You finally reach a wide path, which you ascend for about 100 metres before reaching a pass.

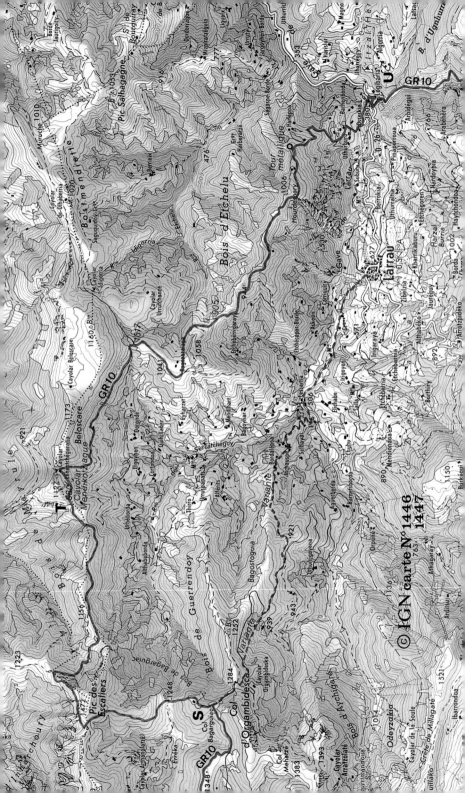

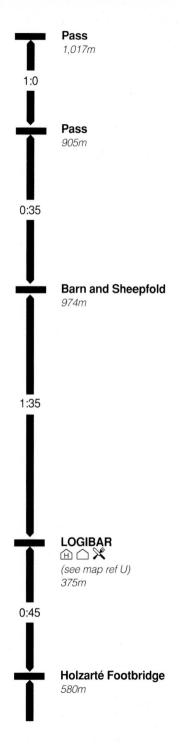

Pass
1,017m

1:0

Pass
905m

0:35

Barn and Sheepfold
974m

1:35

LOGIBAR
⌂ ⌂ ✗
(see map ref U)
375m

0:45

Holzarté Footbridge
580m

From the pass, walk south-west on a path along the crest for 500 metres. It then bears right, encircles an enclosure and heads down. This stretch is usually muddy. You then go over a little spur and down the crest south-eastwards as far as a pass.

Walk up on to the crest, or slightly to the south-west to pass to the right of two nondescript hillocks of 949 and 944 metres. When you reach a pass (940 metres) continue to walk upwards in a south-easterly direction. Bear right to go over a spur at approximately 970 metres, and continue on the level, without losing altitude, towards a meadow bounded by a low wall and some trees. Skirt its lower edge to emerge to the east of a barn and sheepfold.

Pass between these two buildings before taking a good quality path, which first heads north-east and then east. It joins the ridge at 981 metres, where you will find a drinking fountain. Follow the ridge for a few hundred metres on the level, and then drop down towards the north-east, directly to the right of the fence, which it leaves once and for all. At the 853 metre level, near a metal tower used for pigeon shooting, and a house, the road divides. Take the right-hand fork, which plunges southwards. At 560 metres, leave the path, which is often closed by a gate, and follow the traverse to the right to join a dirt road. Follow this for 30 metres until you come to another traverse on the left. At another fork, turn right, to rejoin the dirt road. Walk down the road for several hundred metres to reach Logibar.

Follow the D26 for 100 metres westwards and, immediately after the bridge, take a track to the left which ends 300 metres further on. Cross the De la Mouline bridge, then immediately bear right to take a footpath going up the right bank of the Holzarté river. You walk up the bank, rising higher and higher above the gorges as far as the Holzarté footbridge over the Olhadubi waterfall.

Cross the footbridge and take a path to the left, which climb in zigzags through the Holzarté wood. After 730 metres you are on a terrace. From here follow the ledge to the left (south-

51

© IGN carte N° 1447

east). The path becomes narrower by degrees and at times, very muddy, providing views of the gorges far below to the left. You gain height slightly and cross first one stream, and then another on stepping stones, and finally the Olhadubi Bridge.

Olhadubi Bridge
(see map ref V)
840m

Continue to the left (north) on the path which runs almost horizontally along the right side of the Olhadubi ravine. The GR10 makes virtually a complete circuit around the ravine. Cross a stream and then 100 metres further on, a mere trickle. A short while later, (IGN map ref 855) turn right on to a footpath. At first you walk parallel to the path you have just left, then you climb rapidly northwards. The path reaches a pass (990 metres) between a rounded hill to the left (see IGN map ref 999), and the Cayolar d'Ardakhotchia (shepherds' hut) 200 metres to the right (south-east). Cross the track leading to the hut and scramble eastwards up the grassy and then stony brow of a hill. There is no path. Below, to the south-east, you can see a road which you could join and follow from the Cayolar d'Abarrakia (shepherds' hut) at 1,200 metres, for several hundred metres to the south-east. In good weather use the old footpath, which winds below the road through the Saratzé wood to the shepherds' hut of the same name.

Saratzé Cayolar
1,205m

Walk up its access track to join the road that you glimpsed earlier. Keep to this road, leading south, on the level. After 2 kilometres leave the Olhaberria Cayolar (1,230 metres) to your right, and, a little further on, the Iguéloua Hut (1,230 metres) with a new building, to the left. After another 200 metres leave the road, just before a bridge, and walk up to the left (east), on the right side of a grassy depression. There is no path, and almost no markers. Go over the ridge that separates the communes of Larrau and Saint-Engrâce to the Col d'Anhaou.

Col d'Anhaou
1,383m

Alternative route, from the Anhaou Pass to Sainte-Engrâce, marked. From the pass walk south-east down a site path, or, preferably take a parallel footpath, which passes the Sohotolhatzé Cayolar (1,320 metres), and runs horizontally across pasture land, leaving

1:0

1:45

1:0

the track and the Cayolar d'Anhaou (1,280 metres) to the left. Keep along the southern edge of a wood, and go diagonally southwards down fairly steep grassy slopes, which overlook the southern end of the Kakouéta Gorge. There are many tracks but no proper footpath. You should, therefore, take great care, particularly when there is fog. You reach the Kakouéta footpath (1,125 metres) 40 minutes after leaving the Anhaou Pass. Follow the footpath southwards. After an hour's walking you cross the Kakouéta torrent at an altitude of 950 metres. Climb up again, eastwards, through the forest to reach the Cayolar de Larrégorry (1,227 metres) after another hour's walk. From there take a forest path downhill heading in a general north-north-easterly direction for 6 kilometres, which brings you to Saint Engrâce's stream and the D113 road at an altitude of 563 metres. You can then either cross the stream to continue on the steep path that, in 15 minutes, reaches Sainte-Engrâce, level with the Hôtel Hondagneu; or you can continue along the road, on the left bank, going eastwards, to reach Senta (near the church), thus avoiding the D113.

3:0

SAINTE-ENGRACE
(see overleaf)

Col d'Anhaou

Do not take the vehicular track that leads south-east, but instead descend eastwards in a huge, grassy bowl. At an altitude of 1,315 metres, you come across some trees and have to go round to the left to find an almost horizontal path (1,120 metres) below the confluence of two streams. This path crosses the grassy and quite steep hillside. You go over a spur at 1,070 metres and bear north-north-eastwards to pass over a hilltop on a shelf (1,040 metres). Then walk down a slope covered in grass and bracken heading north. At an altitude of 960 metres, you reach a path in the form of a hairpin bend. Follow it downwards in a south-easterly direction until you reach a dirt road.

1:0

Dirt road
(see map ref W)
909m

Walk north along this road for several metres to join a path, which plunges to the right (north). Cut across a stream near the buildings marked `Granges' on the map. Go right, (east), and then, 500 metres further on, walk

0:30

55

©IGN carte N°1447

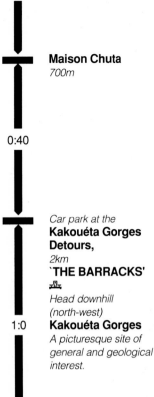

Maison Chuta
700m

0:40

Car park at the
**Kakouéta Gorges
Detours,**
2km
`THE BARRACKS'

*Head downhill
(north-west)*
1:0 **Kakouéta Gorges**
*A picturesque site of
general and geological
interest.*

CALLA

**EGLISE DE SAINTE-
ENGRACE**

(see map ref X)
630m
*Beautiful 19th century
church.*

down a sunken path bounded by a low wall. The path bears right, passes the house called Drounda, and comes out at Maison Chuta.

Go into this farm's courtyard and down part of its approach road, which leads to `The Barracks'. After 1 kilometre, take the stile over the fence and walk round the edge of a meadow down to the Berreteretchia House (540 metres). Leave it to your left and walk down the meadow on the north side to find a path which plunges down towards the torrent. You come to it at the Pont d'Enfer (Hell's Bridge). Cross over and walk up to join the D113 again, a few hundred metres downhill from the car park at the Kakouéta Gorges.

Continue up the road to the south-east towards Calla (see left). After 1,500 metres (or 3.5 kilometres from the Kakouéta Gorges) you reach the Sainte-Engrâce Church.

Alternative route from Sainte-Engrâce to Arette-la-Pierre-Saint Martin, 4 hr 30 min, not marked. This alternative is recommended in bad weather: rain spoils the enjoyment of the long climb through the Lèche wood and, higher up, the fog can be particularly treacherous. In the absence of visibility, it is also pointless to climb up to the Pierre-Saint-Martin (St. Martin's Stone), which is higher than the resort. Several hundred metres to the west of the church, take a forest road to the left (north-east) that runs behind the pelota court and rises roughly eastwards. You can follow the road as far as the Col de Suscousse or you can avoid 3 kilometres of tarmac by branching off just at the end of a hairpin bend (950 metres), about 4.5 kilometres from Sainte-

57

© IGN carte N°1447-1547

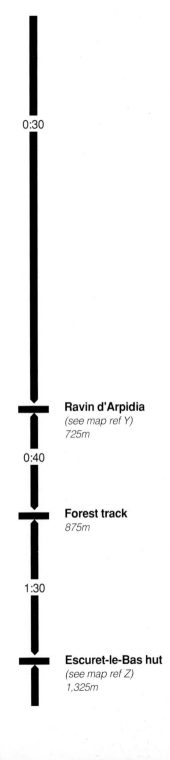

0:30

Ravin d'Arpidia
(see map ref Y)
725m

0:40

Forest track
875m

1:30

Escuret-le-Bas hut
(see map ref Z)
1,325m

Engrâce to take a valley road rising eastwards as far as the Col de Suscousse (1,210 metres). This stretch takes 2 hr 30 min from Sainte Engrâce. Again you have a choice. You can take the road to D'Arette-la-Pierre-Saint-Martin, but it is preferable, and certainly more pleasant, to follow the yellow and red markers which lead south from the Suscousse Pass. Walk uphill through a forest as far as the edge of a coomb, and then go down through clearing to the Cagastié Coomb. You then climb up again on the opposite face and, as you leave the forest, reach Soum de Soudet (1,542 metres) 1 hr 30 minutes after leaving Suscousse Pass. You now follow the crest till you reach the D132 road. Stay on it, heading south to the resort of Arette-la-Pierre-Saint-Martin, which you reach after 30 minutes.

From the church follow a path, which descends first eastwards and then towards the south. Cross a small bridge (590 metres) and walk south-east up a stony path for 10 minutes or so. At 630 metres, take a footpath, which zigzags up towards the south. A little higher up, fork left (south-east). You pass under an electric power line and come to the bottom of the Arpidia ravine.

Follow the bottom of the ravine south-east for about 10 minutes. Leave this defile for a footpath on the left (north), which then rises up to the north-east through the Lèches wood, where felled trees cause a slight diversion to the left. Soon, you reach a forest track.

Go up the unsurfaced track, which is closed to motor traffic. It is crossed several times, by the old footpath and ends at a curious drinking trough divided into 8 compartments and decorated with a concrete bust of the `Protector', signed by Barétoun artist. In a few minutes you reach the edge of the forest and, after you have passed the last markings on the trees, the GR heads south-east over grass to the ruins of the Escuret-le-Bas hut.

Alternative route from Escuret-le-Bas hut to the Station at Arette-la-Pierre-Saint-Martin, 1 hr 45 min. This route avoids climbing the

© IGN carte N°1447-1547

eroded fort. Take what used to be a shepherds' path and walk in an easterly direction. You cross a forest and join the D132 road. Follow this to reach the resort of Arette-la-Pierre-Saint-Martin.

From the dilapidated hut, the GR10 goes up and mainly to the south through the pasture land with no footpath but, instead, markers on the chalk rocks. You will find a track coming from the De Féas hut, which is to your left. Go up this track heading south; it takes you just above the Cabane du Coup.

1:30

Cabane du Coup
1,522m,
View of the Pic d'Orhy.

Follow the footpath as it climbs in hairpins southwards. At a height of 1,740 metres, you reach a crest to the south-west of the Soum de Lèche (1,739 metres). You circle the Soum de Lèche to the south, walking in a south-easterly direction. First you come to the D'Escuret hut and then, continuing along the ridge, the Col de la Pierre Saint-Martin.

1:0

Col de la Pierre Saint-Martin
1,760m. Panoramic view of the Pic d'Anie massif;
entrance (closed)
to the Lepineux gorge, 728
metres deep; tarmac road
linking Isaba in Spain to the
French resort of La Pierre
Saint-Martin and to Arette;
junction with the Haute
Randonnée Pyrénéenne
(north-east)

Walk down the tarmac road on the French side. After about 1,200 metres go right, ignoring the old markers for the GR10 which used to go round the south side of the Turon d'Arlas. Instead, go to the west of this small hill (1,762 metres). About 200 metres before you come to the tarmac, the GR crosses two ski-lifts, and goes up to the right on a track which passes to the north of the Turon d'Arlas, passing the Customs Post below on the left. When you come to the Eaux de la Pierre-Saint-Martin building, descend eastwards, to the resort of Arette-la-Pierre-Saint-Martin

0:45

ARETTE-LA-PIERRE-SAINT-MARTIN
⌂ ♨
(see map ref 1)
1,640m
Ski resort with extensive
view of the Plaine de Lacq
and the Pics d'Anie, d'Arlas
and Soumcouy; a
departure point for the
Vallée de Varétous tours.

From the resort of Arette-la-Pierre-Saint-Martin take a stony road southwards to the De Pescamou shepherds' hut. After a while, leave the road and head eastwards passing under the De Pescamou chair lift. Now walk down a ski piste for 50 metres and then go right for the western end of the Arres de Camlong.

0:50

Arres de Camlong
Large plateau of cracked
and fissured calcareous

The path winds among the rocks, follows a gorge and, after an opening in the rocks, reaches one pass (1,930 metres) and then a

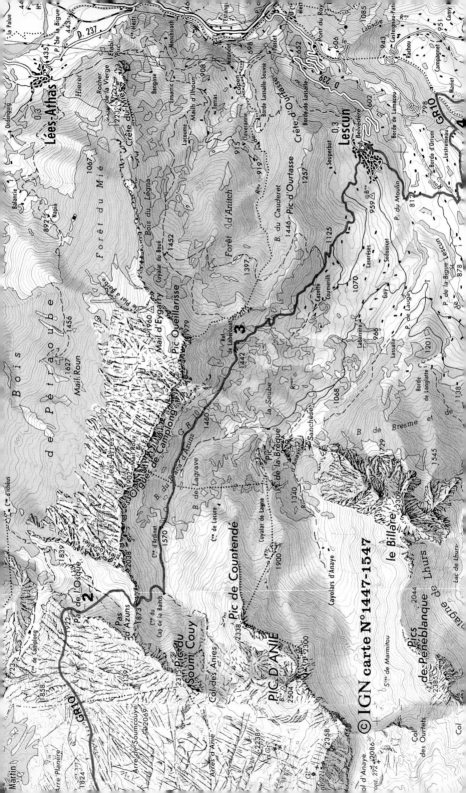

© IGN carte N°1447-1547

1:40 *rock, characteristic of the area. Many salamanders on rainy days.*

Pas de l'Osque
(see map ref 2)
1,922m
Access to the northern ridge of the Soumcouy peak.
0:15

Pas d'Azuns
1,873m.
Beautiful view over the Oloron Plain and surrounding peaks of Soumcouy, Anie and Countendé.
1:10

REFUGE DE LABÉROUAT
△
(see map ref 3)
1,442m
0:25

GÎTE D'ÉTAPE 'RANDONNÉES PYRÉNÉES'
△
From the gîte, there are several shortcuts to the village of Lescun.
1:0

LESCUN
△ ⚓
900m;
beautiful setting in amphitheatre of calcareous peaks.
1:0

second one (1,900 metres). From here, there is a beautiful view over the mountains of the Aspe valley. After a gap, cross a ledge of cracked rock. The footpath overlooks the Camlong pasture land. Next, a steep path in the form of a staircase leads to the Pas de l'Osque.

Take a footpath on the grassy hillside, first to the south-east and then southwards until you come to the Pas d'Azuns.

Descend towards the huts in Azuns, called the `Cap de Baitch' huts (1,689 metres), where you can find water and rock crystals. Walk down a gentle slope towards the east and go through the Braca d'Azuns, which is a beechwood. As you leave the wood there is a wonderful view to the south of the Billare Peak and the Plateau de Sanchèze. Go down to the Refuge de Labérouat.

Go down along the stony road which leads to the Gîte d'étape. You can take a shortcut.

From the Place de la Mairie, to the right of the war memorial, take a street, then a tarmac road going down to the Pont du Moulin (812 metres), which enables you to cross the Lescun Stream. From the right bank take the shortcut which climbs steeply through the woods and comes out at a crossroads, marked `Porte du Parc National' (entrance gate to the national park). Follow the tarmac road southwards. After 200 metres, take a footpath, which crosses the old road several times and comes out on to a wide tarmac path on the level. Turn left and head north-east. After 600

© IGN carte N° 1547

metres you come to a footpath heading north. Follow it to the Lestremeau Farm.

Lestremeau Farm
(seep map ref 4)
1,021m

0:45

View of the Lescun amphitheatre and the Aspe valley.

Go through the farm and cross the Brennère stream. Take the footpath on the left (north-east) which crosses a beautiful beech forest and circles the spur that separates the Brennère and the Lhers valleys. As you leave the forest, the horizontal footpath runs above the Lhers plateau and its irrigation network. Go down to the left and cross the Labadie stream at the southern end of the hamlet of Lhers.

Lhers
997m
18th century chapel.

Detour. Follow the Lhers Road south to join a shepherds' path, which leads to the Col de Sahoubathou. There a path made by the National Park authorities allows you to go south-east to reach Lake d'Arlet and then down to the Forges d'Abel (Abel's Forges) on the N134 road below the Col du Sompot. Alternatively, you can go north-west to join the Col de Pau and then walk down towards Lescun.

2:0

Cross the tarmac road. Walk up through meadows as far as a new forest track which, to the left, goes down towards the hamlet of Lhers. Go up this track for about 20 minutes and then take a well-mapped-out zigzag footpath to the left. You will be walking alternately through woodland and across open spaces with bilberries. There are excellent views of the Lescun amphitheatre. You reach the Col de Barranq after a steep climb through the forest.

Col de Barranq
1,601m.
Detour
Follow the crest right (south)for 200 metres. On

0:30

leaving the wood you will have a magnificent view of the Aspe valley, the Sesques Massif and the Midi d'Ossau peak

Go down the eastern side of the pass. Take the path zigzagging through the forest and leave it before you reach the semi-ruined Udapet-de-Haut cabin.

Udapet-de-Haut cabin
1,515m

0:10

A beautiful pastoral site; nearby spring; yellow gentians and bilberries.

Descend to the south-south-east, crossing streams, and passing between boulders. The path turns left near the Udapet-de-Bas cabin.

65

© IGN carte N° 1547

UDAPET-DE-BAS CABIN
⌂

(see map ref 5)
1,401m

1:20

Leave the forest by following the hairpin bends of a forest track. There is a beautiful panoramic view of the Aspe valley, the Sesques massif and the villages of Borce and Etsaut, which are almost vertically below you. Continue in wide zigzags through the bracken on the left bank of the river. When you reach a horizontal path, leave it to the right to cross the torrent. The route passes to the north of the Soulé Farm and comes to a tarmac road. By following the road south-south-eastwards for about 600 metres, you come to a camping site created and run by the National Park. After crossing the tarmac road twice, the marked footpath leads to the village of Borce.

BORCE
⌂ Ⅹ ♨

640m
15th and 16th century houses.

Follow the road to the N134. Turn right on to it and continue to Etsaut.

ETSAUT
⌂ ⌂ ♨ ▬

(see map ref 6)
597m

0:50

Take the N134 for 1,800 metres in the direction of Spain until you reach the Cebers Bridge (637 metres). Do not cross it; instead walk along the right bank of the Aspe river on a tarmac road. After 800 metres, at the first bend, leave the road by turning right to join a footpath which ascends through pastures until you reach a rocky spur which it circles. The path at this point acquires the name of Le Chemin de la Mâture (path for the masts).

Chemin de la Mâture
(see map ref 7)
788m
This man-made path was carved out of a smooth, vertical, calcareous wall in the 18th century for transporting of tree trunks destined to become ships' masts. It overlooks the narrow Hell's Gorge, in whose depths the Sescoué River thunders. Opposite is the 19th century Portalet Fort for political prisoners.

0:50

The GR10 follows this path. After several hundred metres you emerge into the open. This next section may, at times, cause vertigo, but the path is always wide and well marked. A fairly rough upward climb brings you out on a rocky crest. Here the path encircles a promontory, which widens to form the Plateau de la Baigt de Saint-Cours.

© IGN carte N°1547

Plateau de la Baigt de Saint-Cours
1,100m

At the far end of the plateau the Path of the Mâture crosses to the left bank of the torrent (the bridge has been demolished) and disappears into the forest. Stay on the right bank and follow a steep footpath to the left, which joins the access path to two share-cropping farms, Borde de Rouglan and Borde de Passette, which are inhabited in summer. After the second farm, you enter thinned-out woodland and continue walking along the torrent's right bank until you reach the Cabane de la Baigt de Saint-Cours.

1:50

Cabane de la Baigt de Saint-Cours
1,560m
The hut marks the GR10's point of entry into the Parc National des Pyrénées Occidentales.

Take a National Park footpath, which follows first the right bank of the torrent and then the left. You climb gradually over grassland towards the south, leaving to your left the rocky cliff which marks the floor of the amphitheatre. To the north you can see the silhouettes of the Pic de Sesques and the Capéran de Sesques. Continue to walk southwards until you come to the Col de la Hourquette de Larry.

1:40

Hourquette de Larry
2,055m
National Park footpath to Peyrenère

From the pass to the Refuge d'Ayous, the path of the GR10 coincides with that of the *Haute Randonnée Pyrénéenne*. Take the footpath to the east. After going uphill for a short way you reach the Col d'Ayous.

0:30

Col d'Ayous
(see map ref 8)
2,185m
Magnificant view of Pic du Midi d'Ossau; easy 30 minutes ascent to Pic d'Ayous (2,288 metres).

Descend on a good footpath to Lake Gentau.

0:20

LAKE GENTAU
(One of the Lacs d'Ayous)
⌂
1,947m.
Departure point for Col and Pic des Moines (2,349m), or the Bersau and Casterau Lakes route, joining GR10 at Bious Bridge or continuing to Pic du Midi d'Ossau..
Detour, *Tour of the Pic du Midi. Some 400m later the tour branches off to the right. See p.81*

The footpath follows the lake, at a distance of some hundred metres from the northern shore, comes to Lake Mey (1,914 metres) and continues along the left bank of the overflow stream from these two lakes. You should cross the overflow outlet and climb up the sharp rise at the south-east end. From here there is a good view over Lake Roumassot and the Ossau Peak. Descend, via hairpin bends, beside the spillway until you reach Lake Roumassot. Take a diagonal path through four meadows to the edge of a forest (1,704 metres).

1:40

© IGN carte N°1547-1647

Detour, *150m*
CAMP LONG D'AYOUS
⌂
Head north.

Continue downwards, crossing the forest to the Plaine de Bious (1,560 metres). Take the track heading north-eastwards through a wood, passing close to the Bious torrent. Cross the torrent via a concrete bridge. You pass close to a spring, which is cool all the year round. On your way down you have a view over Lake Bious-Artigues. Walk towards the lake. After a while, you come to the car park.

LAKE BIOUS-ARTIGUES
⌂ 𝕏 ⛱
(see map ref 9)
1,417m
Pic du Midi d'Ossau route.
Detour
𝕏 ⛱
Take D231 for 2 hours.

1:0

Take a shortcut to the hamlet of Gabas.

GABAS
🏠 🚋
1,027m
12th century chapel; centre for Mountain Ecology; excursion centre: Ossau, Arrémoulit, Arriel via the CAF hut at Pombie and Arrémoulit.

0:20

Follow the D934 and its shortcuts towards Spain for approximately 1,600 metres until you reach the hydro-electric power station.

Les Alhas Hydro-Electric Station
(see map ref 10)
1,135m
(Marked as Central électrique d'Artouste on IGN map). 6km along D934, cable car to Artouste (2,067m), and, in summer, to the little train to Lake d'Artouste and CAF hut of Arrémoulit.

1:0

About 50 metres downhill from the tollgate, the GR10 crosses the De Brousset torrent via the Bridge des Alhas. The footpath turns back westwards, almost on the level, then climbs a few hairpins overlooking Gabas. You enter the de Piet forest and head northwards over slight ups and downs. You come to a good, tarmac forest road and stay on it for about 400 metres before reaching a junction with the Corniche des Alhas footpath.

Corniche des Alhas footpath
1,130m
The Des Alhas corniche is crossed by a footpath cut into a granite cliff, overlooking the Du Soussouéou gorge. The

Alternative route. To avoid the corniche, continue along the forest road as it descends in hairpin bends to the Du Goua bridge (966 metres). By continuing west along the road, you join the D934 road at De Hourcq Bridge. Cross the river on this bridge and go up by an unmarked, but well laid out footpath, until you meet the GR10 at the point named below as

© IGN carte N°1547-1647

1:0

path has been damaged from time to time by avalanches and can cause dizziness, as well as being dangerous even though a rail has been provided.

Corniche des Alhas
(see map ref 11)

0:30

The water supply at Soussouéou
1,110m

0:10

De Soussouéou path
First crossroads
1,113m
Hikers coming in the other direction and wanting to avoid Des Alhas corniche, can use the footpath dropping down west to Du Goua Bridge. From here take the forest road going up in hairpin bends to the junction with Corniche des Alhas Footpath.

1:0

De Soussouéou Path
Second crossroads
1,345m

0:30

Horizontal path
from old copper mine
(see map ref 12)
Beautiful view of Cézy cliffs and, on the horizon, of De Sesques massif

the `first crossroads on the De Soussouéou path' (1,113 metres). This loop adds an extra 30 minutes to the route.

The GR10 veers right, leaving the tarmac forest road, to reach the De Piet crossroads (1,092 metres), where it follows a footpath to the right. This climbs upwards and becomes the service path for a subterranean canal, which brings you to the Corniche des Alhas.

Cross the corniche on the narrow vertiginous path cut out of the cliff. Take great care as this can be dangerous. After crossing the Corniche des Alhas, the footpath comes to the Herrana forest with its beautiful beeches and fir trees, and then to the water supply at Soussouéou.

A concrete bridge takes you to the right bank of the Soussouéou. Here the footpath winds under magnificent trees as far as the first crossroads on the De Soussouéou path.

Take the path called De Soussouéou to the right. Cross an almost horizontal plateau dotted with thickets. Then the path climbs in quite steep zigzags up the flank of the Cézy under the trees, crosses the clearing and the De Mouscabarous spring (1,156 metres) and comes to the second crossroads.

Leave on your right the path going up towards the De Soussouéou plain and take a turning to the left towards the De la Tume cliff. Walk along very steep hairpin bends until you leave the forest. Continue along the bottom of a chalk cliff until you reach a copper mine path.

Take the horizontal path to the right, heading east. The path is wide and well marked, passing below the Cézy huts and overlooking the Soussouéou plain. Continue down the path on a gentle and steady slope. After a few hairpin bends you reach Le Coujalet de Hourtanet, and head diagonally north-east

© IGN carte N° 1647

2:50

towards an old iron mine (2,099 metres). The route now heads south on a gentle slope, before turning on a succession of zigzag bends, first on a grassy slope, then through a ravine of red rocks. After a hard climb on scree where the marking may be poor, you reach the Hourquette d'Arre.

1:0

Hourquette d'Arre
(see map ref 13)
2,465m
View towards Amoulat,
Arcizette, Sesques and
Ossau

About 200 metres north of the col, the footpath passes in front of a hunters' hut, which can be used as a temporary shelter. Then, maintaining the same level, it crosses a valley going down to Lake de Lavedan, towards the east, and climbs over a poorly-marked col. The path crosses diagonally to the east, then heads north, descending in quite steep hairpin bends to the ruins of the old iron mining buildings close to the Anglas Lake.

1:30

Anglas Lake
2,068m
There is a fine view of the
Sarrière ridge to the north
and the Latte de Bazen to
the north-east.

The path follows the eastern shore of the lake, crosses its spillway diagonally, and descends in steep zigzags towards the Valentin torrent. The path drops gently to the pastures and passes under the Des Crêtets gondola lift. The route markings end on the chairlift building `the Fil-Neige' 200 metres from Gourette.

1:30

GOURETTE
1,346m.
Winter and summer sports
resort in a circle of high
mountains: Latte de Bazen,
Sanctus, Pic der Ger.
Several marked walking
routes, in particular the
Vallée d'Ossau tour.

Leave Gourette on the N618 heading towards the Col d'Aubisque. About 300 metres after passing the last houses, you turn to the right through a pine wood, skirt two chalets and climb rapidly, past a harnessed stream, to a grassy plateau. From here you have a good view, to the south-west, of the peaks of Ger, Pène Médaa and Pène Sarrière. After continuing almost horizontally, the path passes through a mass of broken stones, and then goes up grassy slopes to the Col de Tortes.

Col de Tortes
(see map ref 14)
1,799m

During the descent from the Col de Tortes, you come across the GR route for the `Tour of the Ossau Valley'. Its yellow and red markers head west, in the direction of the Col d'Aubisque. The footpath drops steadily down through grassland, turns right to follow a ridge dotted with rocks, and comes out at the Route nationale.

0:50

© IGN carte N°1647

Route Nationale 618
1,390m

Take the N618 to the right for approximately 2.5 kilometres.

Alternative route via the Litor huts to the De Saucède Pass. If you want to avoid 3 kilometres of tarmac, and, at the beginning of the season if there is deep snow on the road, you are advised to cross the pastureland below the Litor amphitheatre. This route adds 20 minutes to the time and includes 190 metres of uneven surfaces. Cross the N618 and go down the small valley of the Arbaze as far as the springs at Cap d'Ouzom (1,131 metres). A path leads to the Litor huts and then goes up to the N618, not far from the path on the De Saucède pass.

1:15

Enter the Litor amphitheatre, from where you can see the plain (north) and the Peaks of Gabizos (south). From the milestone on the Ouzom ridge (1,350 metres) separating the departments of the Pyrénées-Atlantiques and the Hautes-Pyrénées walk 650 metres and take a small footpath to the right, which climbs up a fairly steep slope to the Col de Saucède.

Col de Saucède
(see map ref 15).

Take a wide piste on the left for 50 metres which, in 20 minutes, comes out at the pass for road traffic at Soulor (see left).

SOULOR
△ ✗ ☂ ⚓

1:40

Take a track to the right over a slope, passing the ruins of a hut to the left, and following the right bank of a stream. Cross the stream below a shepherd's hut, where you may be able to buy cheese. Climb up the escarpments, crossing grassy slopes suitable for camping. Pass a marshy valley to your right and follow a spur, which narrows and, at the end, lacks grass due to being trampled by cattle. From here there is a view over the Azun valley. Walk diagonally to the right and descend as far as a stream. Follow this along its left bank and cross it when you are level with the first trees. Then take a well-marked path called Queen Hortense. This widens and then follows a road. Leave the road to the left at Moura Farm, return to it, and then finally leave it again to go straight down to the D105 (925 metres). Turn left on to the D105, and walk beside the buildings of the Centre Thébault.

© IGN carte N°1647

Turn right on to a footpath which runs between low walls down to the old bridge.

La Badét Bridge
895m

After a few minutes walk you come to Arrens.

ARRENS
Ⓗ ⌂ ⋀ ▭
878m
15th century church;
Aucun (3km)
church; Bigourdin
museum; departure point
for Lac de Migouélou, the
frontier crest, Gabizos, Pic
du Midi d'Arrens, etc

Walk 2 continues from here. (See page 85.)

Circular walk round the Pic du Midi d'Ossau

The circular walk round the Pic du Midi d'Ossau is an alternative to the Sentier de Grande Randonnée GR10 - Béarne-Etsaut-Gabas - although they follow the same route for about 2 kilometres. It is a moderate mountain route, rising to 2,194 metres at the Col d'Iou and 2,127 metres at the Col de Suzon. In winter, the Tour de l'Ossau is a classic trackless skiing route, which takes a trained skier about 10 hours.

But, summer or winter, the real reason for the tour is to get to know, from all angles, the double purple peaks of the Ossau Massif which tower above two deep valleys. The Tour du Pic du Midi d'Ossau covers only the high plateaus or wide valleys and, for the greater part of the tour, the rocky mass of the Grand Pic (2,884 metres) and the Petit Pic (2,807), can be seen clearly, without any foothills or lower chains of mountains.

Another pleasure awaits the hiker: the whole massif forms part of the Parc National des Pyrénées (the Pyrenean National Park), which includes the entire Ossau Reserve where hunting is forbidden all the year round; several hundred wild goats live there.

Because of the altitude and the likelihood of snow, the tour of the Pic du Midi d'Ossau can only be made between the end of June and the end of October. It can be covered in one long stretch of 8 hours. But the CAF (French Alpine Club) has a hut at Pombie, which is about half way. Here you can break the journey, or at least stop for a rest and some refreshment.

The Tour du Midi d'Ossau was first marked out in 1966, following a rather rough plan and passing over the Col de Peyreget (222 metres). Since then, the National Park has marked out a path covering the same circuit, but going from the east via the Col d'Iou and round the Pic de Peyreget, which affords a beautiful panoramic view of the Anéou amphitheatre and the mountains on the Spanish frontier. Naturally, this route has been adopted by the GR. However, you can go directly to the hut at Pombie via the Peyreget Pass (2,322 metres), where you will have a magnificent view. An even better view can be obtained by climbing up the side of the Pic de Peyreget.

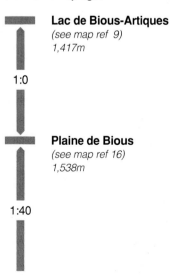

Lac de Bious-Artiques
(see map ref 9)
1,417m

1:0

From the parking place at the end of the D231 take the forest path to the south, which follows the GR10 route and runs along the eastern shore of the lake. Cross over a concrete bridge to the left bank of the Bious torrent. The footpath climbs up through a beautiful pine forest and comes out on the Plaine de Bious.

Plaine de Bious
(see map ref 16)
1,538m

1:40

While the GR10 heads right into the forest, the Tour du Pic du Midi d'Ossau footpath leads slightly to the left to cross the Bious torrent via a concrete bridge. Some distance from the right bank, the path heads south-west, crosses the plain for about 800 metres, and then changes direction first towards the south and then east to traverse the Arazures wood in zigzags. You emerge in the Peyreget valley, where the track is now shared as far as

the Peyreget Lake with that of the Haute Randonnée Pyrénéene. By a gradual ascent southwards you reach the Peyreget Lake.

Peyreget Lake
2,074m

0:20

The Petit Pic (the little peak) increasingly hides the Grand Pic, as the path heads south-east to the Col de l'Iou.

Col de l'Iou
(see map ref 17)
2,194m
This col is not marked on the 1/50,000 IGN map
A fine view of Circque d'Anéou, frontier pass of Pourtalet (1,794m) and Spanish mountains

0:50

The path curves east to encircle the Peyreget Peak (2,487m) and remaining on the flat, leads to the Anéou crossroads.

Anéou Crossroads
(see map ref 18)
2,129m;
not marked on IGN 1/50,000 map; path (1.0 hour) to D934 near Pourtalent Pass.

0:30

The footpath descends gently north and leads towards the Pombie refuge.

Daybreak on Pic du Midi d'Ossau as seen from Refuge d'Ayous

POMBIE REFUGE
⌂ ⋏

(see map ref 19).
2,031m
Starting base for climbs in the Ossau massif.

0:50

The footpath runs along a lake shore and continues westwards, rising slightly, then veering northwards as it descends. First, cross the Grande Raillère Pombie, and then some grazing land before climbing to the Col de Suzon.

Col de Suzon
2,127m.
Departure point for usual ascent of Ossau; Saoubiste (2,261 metres) reached in 30 minutes by walking east

1:40

The path starts by going downhill along, first the right, and then the left banks of the Magnabaigt river as you head towards the valley of the same name. Walk along the base of the De Moundelhs ridge, which gradually obscures the Ossau. You go down close to a waterfall, then follow a gentle slope towards the west through a veritable garden of rhododendrons to the Col Long de Magnabaigt.

Col Long de Magnabaigt
(see map ref 20)
1,655m
Beautiful view over Lavigne Peak, Ger Massif and Massif des Sesques

0:40

By coming down through the Bious Artigues wood to the west, you reach the Bious-Artigues Lake.

THE BIOUS-ARTIGUES LAKE
⌂
1,417m

You rejoin the GR10, near the Club Pyrénéa Sports refuge.

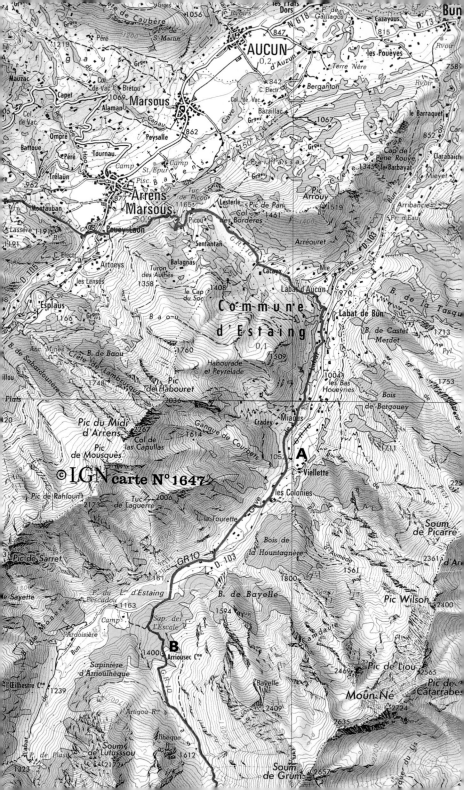

WALK 2

Arrens
878m.
15th century church;
Aucun (3km), Norman
and Gothic style church;
museum of Bigorre folk
art; point of departure for
Lake Migouélo, frontier
ridge, Pic du Midi d'Arrens,
The Gabizos, and
magnificant Balaitous
Massif

The GR10 does not enter the village of Arrens, but takes the Badéte bridge over the mountain stream and bears left on a broad footpath; then it goes to the right through a wicket-gate into the ONF Arboretum, to follow the road, with a short cut through the woods on the left, to the Col des Bordères.

The Shepherd's Collection

1:0

Tourists going up the Azun valley from Argelès-Gazost to Arrens on the N618 can visit the interesting Lavedan museum of rural ethnology. An old shepherd with a deep affection for his region has assembled items showing the full range of rural valley life in the old days. Visitors can see everything used for dealing with ewes' wool, from the `estelhans', the shears, to the `débadé', the spools for the wool made of twisted branches, and beautifully carved shepherds' crooks. Some items are entirely simple, such as the `landéa', a young pine stem with its twigs forming a thoroughly functional whisk to stir the clotted milk. Then there is the `penté dé clé', the weaving frame with its dozens of reed strips on a wooden frame, which attracts the connoisseur's eye. There is also the extraordinary shepherds' hut, a sort of coffin-shaped edifice where the shepherds sheltered from wolves on summer nights.

From `*Visages de la Campagne Française'*, Reader's Digest.

Col des Bordères
1,150m.
Vast grassy plateau, with
houses and farm buildings.

0:30

Follow the road across the plateau, heading south-east. As the road begins to descend, about 50 metres from a wooden cross, turn right on to a shady path along the left bank of a stream. Cross the road twice, and then follow it to Estaing.

Estaing
990m

0:40

Take the D103 up the valley for 4 kilometres to a lake. To avoid the narrow and very busy road, keep to the right at the first bridge - the left bank of the stream - then come back to the access road leading to Viellette.

Viellette
(see map ref A)
1,075m

Follow the road for 800 metres and take the Escalère bridge back to the left bank for 1 kilometre, as far as the Counseilhs bridge where you return to the road and 200 metres

© IGN carte N° 1647

0:40

1:0

LAC D'ESTAING
⌂
1,161m

3:0

CABANE D'ARRIOU-SEC
⌂
(see map ref B)
1,400m

BARBAT CABANE
⌂
1859m

Col d'Illhéou
2,242m

0:45

LAC D'ILLHÉOU
⌂
(see map ref C)
1,975m

Detour, *1 day,*
WALLON OR MARCADAU MOUNTAIN REFUGE HUTS:
⌂

further on turn left on to a footpath. This soon brings you to the hotel, and then to the lake at Estaing.

Follow the road along the lake for 500 metres, then turn left on to the footpath up into the Escale pine forest (ONF). This crosses a driveway from the Centre d'Acceuil (information centre) three times, and then leads to the Cabane d'Arriou-Sec.

After rounding a sharp spur the footpath carries on south-east across gentle grassy slopes above the right bank of a stream. At the bottom of the `cirque' cross several small streams and, at the foot of a steep rocky outcrop, at an altitude of about 1,850 metres, you pass a valley on the right (see left).

Curve left round a hollow, and climb up a footpath, which runs along a 'corridor' heading south-east. This takes you past a small lake on your left, to the very large, fairly level, grassy area of the Col d'Illhéou.

From this large and reasonably flat pass, carry on eastwards. At an altitude of 2,185 metres you pass to the left of two huts; one built of stone and the other painted metallic green. This brings you into the National Park, which is responsible for maintaining the GR10 waymarking. Follow the left side of a small ravine. To the left (north-east) the national park footpath heads up to the higher end of the cable railway from the Lis de Cauterets. However, you continue downwards, turning to the right at 2,073 metres. Cross a stream and then a grassy shelf, with a ruined cabin and a marshy spring; after a long fine walk you reach the spot where water runs out of the Lac d'Illhéou.

Follow a track which is semi-suitable for vehicles and goes down to the north, passing above the Lac Noir. The track then turns left, where as the GR10 continues straight on to a grassy hollow, and then to two small passes where there is water. Beyond the second of

© IGN carte N° 1647

Walk for fit and experienced walkers; rejoin GR10, either from Pont d'Espagne, or at Les Oulettes de Gaube.

1:15

these there are two rocky stretches, which require some care in damp conditions. They are known as the Escale d'Illhéou and were feared by shepherds in the past. You emerge on to a stony track. Follow it for 50 metres, then descend steeply across scree, cross the track again, and continue across the long slopes of the Arralhé Blu, with its springs and view of the Escale waterfall. Pick up the track again, just before a modern culvert. Keep to the right bank, passing between a spring and a small, ancient bridge over the Illhéou mountain stream, known as the Pôntou dets Sahucs.

Pôntou dets Sahucs
(see map ref D)
1,481m

After fording the Dets Sahucs spring, turn left and follow the route down some very steep hairpin bends over the steep rocks by the Illhéou waterfall. Again, the slope above the water requires some care. The bank soon opens out and walking becomes easier as you proceed over the grassy banks of a former hay-field irrigation canal. These hay-fields spread out across the great Cambasque basin, down which you soon descend. This area overlooks the Courbet valley which marks the end, on the opposite side, of the road from Cauterets (see left).

0:45

COURBET VALLEY
⌂ ✗

Continue along the old irrigation canal for about 15 minutes, and then follow another canal, which runs parallel to it, until you reach a low dry-stone wall. Now walk along a sheep-track, lined with ash trees until you come to the Granges de Houssat.

Granges de Houssat
1,280m

Pass between two barns and turn down immediately to the left on to a modern road, heading downhill to the left (west). After 100 metres turn right on to a wide track, and then take the old grass Cauterets track. You soon leave this, walking downwards, to the left again, through a copse on a rapidly twisting footpath. Finally, you come out on the road again at the Ferme Basque bridge.

Ferme Basque Bridge
1,116m

Alternative route from Ferme Basque Bridge to GR10 going to Pont d'Espagne. Avoid Cauterets by following the road for 1,200 metres until you pick up the GR10 heading to Pont d'Espagne.

©IGN carte N°1647

0:45

To go down to Cauterets follow the road for just 200 metres, and then turn left on to a track going down the wooded bank of the Cambasque mountain stream in steep hairpin bends. This brings you to the Séqués Lane and then the Mamelon Vert Avenue. Follow this for 250 metres, as far as the `Quartier de la Futaie' steps, leading up to the right to the Pont de'Espagne. The Place Centrale of Cauterets is 100 metres away to the left.

CAUTERETS

🏠 ⌂ Å 🚐 🛈

(see map ref E)
913m
Holiday spa resort at head of four high valleys; their waterfalls provide a magnificent spectacle all the year round

From Cauterets walkers can choose between two routes to Luz-Saint-Sauveur: 1) via the Col de Riou, 1,949 metres, 6 hours' walking on an easy footpath, open from May to October; this route is affected by the construction work for a road and ski resort. 2) via the Hourquette d'Ossoue, 2734 metres, and Gavarnie, 1365 metres, three days' walking on a route which has no major difficulties between 14 July and 30 September, but demands a reasonable degree of fitness; some of the steep slopes are under snow throughout the year and the sheer drops can appear quite vertiginous. The demands of these three days have their reward, however, in the beauty of the area, particularly at the foot of the north face of the Vignemale.

1:0

Alternative route from Cauterets to Luz-Saint-Sauveur via the Col de Riou (1,949 metres); 6 hours on an easy footpath; open from May to October. From Cauterets, take a footpath to the left of the Thermes de César (Caesar's Baths), up hairpin bends through the wood to the Pauze-Vieux hot baths, at 1,029 metres, where there is a view over Cauterets. Turn left on to the road which runs along the mountain side. At a forest hut, leave the footpath, which heads off to the right and continue along the road and across the stream. The tarmac road turns into a broad track. After two hairpin bends you come to the Chalet de la Reine Hortense.

CHALET DE LA REINE HORTENSE

🍽

1,211m

Pass behind the chalet and head north-east; to the left there is a view down the valley towards Lourdes. As you enter the wood, follow a drive for 500 metres, and then turn left on to the old footpath. This soon crosses the drive and, after several hairpin bends, reaches

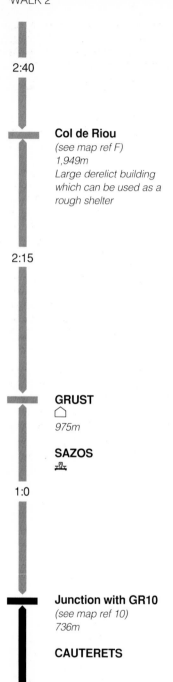

2:40

2:15

1:0

Col de Riou
(see map ref F)
1,949m
Large derelict building
which can be used as a
rough shelter

GRUST
⌂
975m

SAZOS
⚒

Junction with GR10
(see map ref 10)
736m

CAUTERETS

a clearing, at 1,475 metres. Below and to the left is the Laplagne barn. Continue upwards at an angle heading first towards the right and then towards the left, as you climb the rocky outcrop of the Riou plateau. Circle the plateau to the right; increasingly tight hairpin bends take you to the Col de Riou.

Descend in a north-east direction, then follow the route as it takes a wide loop and veers south-west. You pass the double supports of the ski-lift, cross a stream, and come to an area, which is marred by ski-track development work. Continue until you reach a flat parking area. From here to Grust the road cuts across the GR eight times; after the final crossing, take the footpath, directly ahead of you. This provides a shortcut to the right down to Bayesse, where you meet the road again. Cross it and take the path above it, which once more brings you back to the road, at a point, 100 metres upstream from the bridge over the Aulian stream (1,439 metres). Follow the road for 300 metres and turn right on to a shortcut, which crosses the road twice, heading east. You pass beneath two electricity cables before reaching the village of Grust.

Continue down the road; at the second hairpin bend take the footpath on the left, which leads to the village of Sazos (see left).

Walkers seeking a rapid way down to Luz can follow the road for 40 minutes and pick up the GR10 in the middle of Saint Sauveur, or at the Egalité Bridge. Those wanting to go on to Gavarnie, or to Luz along footpaths (1 hour) should take the lane to the right (south-west) in Sazos, and then the footpath south-east across the road, and along the hillside above the Luz basin to the hamlet of Agnouède, beyond which it joins the GR10.

To reach Luz-Saint-Sauveur, or carry on along the GR10 to Barèges, follow the markings to the north; those to the south lead to Gavarnie.

The GR10 to Luz-Saint-Sauveur goes via la Hourquette d'Ossoue (2,734 metres) and Gavarnie (1,365 metres).This route takes 3 days and presents no particular problems between mid July and the end of September.

However, you should be reasonably fit; some of the steep slopes are under snow throughout the year and the sheer drops can be vertiginous, but the reward lies in the beauty of the area, particularly at the foot of the Vignemale's north face.

In Cauteret's Futaie district (see map ref 1) take the steps up on to a footpath which climbs up in hairpin bends. Do not take short cuts, as you will damage the hillside. This is a path for those taking the waters, through a magnificent beech wood to the Péguère Forêt Domaniale (National Forest). This is a model example of the 19th century forester Demontzey's plan, as at Luz and Barèges and in the Alps, to protect villages and valleys from devastation by floods and avalanches, and also to maintain the quality of the soil in the mountains. The GR10 crosses the wide Cambasque road and carries on gently upwards through the forest on an ONF footpath to the Thermes (hot springs) de la Raillère.

0:30

THERMES DE LA RAILLÈRE
✗ ⚓

Views over beautiful waterfalls; on the left the Lutour cascade, on the right the Jéret mountain stream.

1:30

Above the bridge over the Jéret stream cross a small open space. On the right you will see the National Park footpath. The GR10 shares this footpath, past a sequence of famous waterfalls, to the Pont d'Espagne.

PONT D'ESPAGNE
🏠 ✗

(see map ref 2)
1,496m
Notable setting at the confluence of the Gaube and Marcadau mountain streams

Detour, *2hr 35 mins*
REFUGE DU CLOT
◻

and
WALLON REFUGE
1,866m
◻

Detour, (see left). Follow the road past the back of a hotel. After about 800 metres across flat ground, behind a large rock, you find the chalet-refuge (see left). To rejoin the GR10 at the Lac de Gaube, cross the Marcadau stream via two bridges, one after the other, and follow the footpath leading up to the

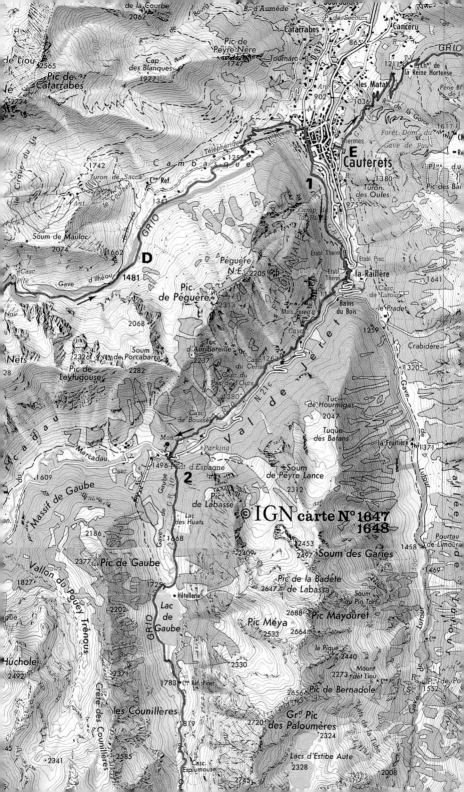

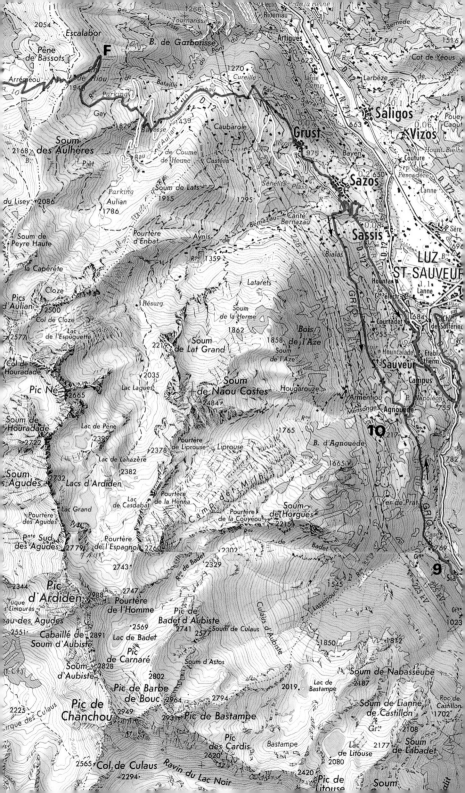

upper chairlift station. To continue to the Wallon Refuge follow the footpath from the Clot chalet along the left bank of the Marcadau stream to the Cayan bridge (1,630 metres). Cross to the right bank, the Park footpath, and at the next bridge, Estalounqué, (1,712 metres) return to the left bank and carry on upwards. The path runs above the Marcadau stream and reaches, on a level stretch, a footbridge. Do not cross this, but carry on heading west, keeping to the same side of the stream, for another 15 minutes, until you reach the Wallon refuge.

0:50

Detour, *1 day,*
OULETTES DE GAUBE
REFUGE

Detour, (see left). Fit mountaineers can rejoin the GR10 at the Oulettes de Gaube (CAF) refuge via the Col d'Arratille, the Rio Ara valley (in Spain), and the Col des Mulets. This is a National Park route which should only be undertaken in fine weather.

Cross the Pont d'Espagne and, 50 metres further on, after a small bridge, turn right on to a fairly steep, but very clearly marked footpath up through beautiful fir trees. The path comes out at the Lac de Gaube.

Lac de Gaube
1,725m

Cross the lake outflow by a footbridge; do not take the wide footpath on the right which leads to the Pont d'Espagne upper chairlift station. Instead, walk i along the lake's west bank, and then along the left bank of the mountain stream. Do not take the first bridge to the left, but a little further on, cross the stream by a second bridge, just below a small gorge. Immediately afterwards the path leads up to the Cabane de Pinet.

0:20

Cabane de Pinet
1,783m

Continue up the right bank of the stream to the sharp rise at the Esplumouse waterfall, at 1,949 metres. The slope becomes more gentle, and the path crosses the Oulettes de Gaube stream by a footbridge.

0:50

Footbridge
1,980m.
View over the Pique
Longue du Vignemale.

Carry on along the river's left bank, cross the Chabarrou stream and, after a small defile, you come out on to the Petites Oulettes plateau. Follow a track along the right edge of the plateau to avoid marshy pasture land. At the far end follow the left bank of the stream. Do not cross it, instead climb up on the granite escarpment. This leads out on to a

0:40

level shoulder; turn left and cross a stream by its footbridge. Shortly afterwards the path leads to the Refuge des Oulettes de Gaube.

REFUGE DES OULETTES DE GAUBE
⌂

(see map ref 3)
2,151m
View to the north face of Vignemale (3,298 metres)

Detour, *1 day,*
WALLON REFUGE
⌂

1:10

Detour, (see left). From here, if you are walking from east to west it is possible to reach the Wallon refuge by crossing the Col des Mulets, the Rio Ara valley (in Spain) and the Col d'Arratille. This route requires a full day of fine weather, and the footpath, kept up by the National Park, is for fit mountaineers.

Leaving the Oulettes de Gaube refuge, turn left on to the footpath heading up and across above the Oulettes du Vignemale plateau (south-east), and then on, via many hairpin bends, to the Centenaire fountain and the fork at the Col d'Araillé.

Fork at the Col d'Araillé
2,435m

Detour,
CAUTERETS

The footpath on the left (north-east) goes past the Col d'Araillé, returning to Cauterets via the Estom lake, the Lutour valley, La Fruitière, and Les Bains

1:15

Take the footpath to the right (south-east), which crosses large areas of scree and frozen snow, then climbs up via wide hairpin bends to the Hourquette d'Ossoue.

Hourquette d'Ossoue
2,734m.
Col between the Guabe and Ossoue valleys. Views over the peaks to the Cirque de Gavar nie.

Climb up to the right (south-west), over a large saddle, with sheer drops to the right, then bear left along the edge of a lip above a glacier. Walkers who suffer from vertigo should not attempt this otherwise easy ascent to the summit.

0:10

Detour, *1 hr,*
Ascent of the Petit Vignemale
3,032m

Take the footpath leading off to the left (east). You will be able to see a refuge perched on a small hillock at the bottom of a stony and snowy valley. A short walk brings you to the Refuge Bayssellance.

99

© IGN carte N° 1648

REFUGE BAYSSELLANCE
⌂

(see map ref 4)
2,651m
This is the highest refuge in the Pyrenees; traditional starting point for the ascent of Vignemale (3,298 metres), via the Ossoue glacier (ropes, ice-axes, crampons).

From the Bayssellance take the good National Park footpath downhill. This rounds the ridge of the Petit Vignemale, then veers first south-west and then east on a tight bend to the left. Leave the clearly marked footpath to the glacier and Vignemale to your right.

2 :0 **Grottes de Bellevue**
240m
Carved out a century ago. They have no amenities, but can be used for shelter.

Carry on along hairpin bends past the Grottes (caves) de Bellevue (2,420 metres). Carry on down the hairpin bends into the deep gorge, known as the `barranco d'Assoue', with its frequent frozen snow-fields and waterfalls. The steep slopes, hard snow, and stretches along ledges demand care from those unaccustomed to such walking, particularly in bad weather. However, the path is always broad and clear. It leads to the level area of the Oulétes d'Ossoue.

OULÉTES D'OSSOUE
⌂
1,866m

1:50

Cross to the left bank via a concrete culvert and follow the bank, then the barrage of the Ossoue dam, which takes you to a hillock with a hut on it. Do not take the track to the left, which leads into a road and goes down to Gavarnie (8 kilometres). Instead, at the foot of the dam take the footbridge to the right. From here the footpath leads up the hillside (1,825 metres) to the south. It is well marked as it crosses steep slopes and ravines for 20-30 minutes before coming to the Lourdes terraces where there is a hut up above which is often used by shepherds. Soon after this you cross the Canaou mountain stream, by a footbridge, and continue walking almost on the level for several kilometres. Next you head first north and then east across grasslands which at first are nearly flat and then become steeper. The path, however, is a ledge 300 metres above the Assoue valley.

Cabane de Saussé-Dessus
(see map ref 5)
1,900m

Take the footbridge across the Saoussé, and then continue still on the level, across grassy areas, which are ideal for camping. In front of you (north) there are impressive chalky escarpments rising from the left side of the valley. The path then veers gradually to the east. You cross several streams or springs and leave the National Park at an altitude of 1,906 metres, before reaching steeper and more wooded slopes. The route now follows a more varied course, which requires caution early in the season if there is snow, beneath the Pouey Arraby escarpments. Beyond the ruined cabin of Tousaous (not Toussus as on the IGN map: `tousaous' or `tozals' are rocky peaks) the path crosses a vast, grassy, hummocky glacis which ends in a cliff-face to the north: it is, therefore, dangerous to stray to the left. The level area is edged intermittently with a fence for the safety of the livestock. Soon after passing a ravine, where there are year-round springs, and before a row of stones set in the grass, you will reach, on the right, the good quality Espécières footpath.

1:0

Sentier des Espécières
1,783m

Detour, *30 mins*
CENTRE COMMUNAL D'HÉBERGEMENT
🏠 ✕

Take the Espécières footpath to the right (south), to meet the road from Gavarnie to Port de Gavarnie via the Vallée des Espécières. Walk up the road (south); the Centre is on the road.

0:45

The GR10 continues along the Serre (ridge) des Tousaous to the east and then down across the last hummocks. It is dangerous to stray to the left (north-east) as there are vertical drops. Walk downwards via several hairpin bends to the road. Turn left and walk beneath the imposing Serre cliff, until you reach the first hairpin bend. Leave the road to curve round it to the left, heading down to the Prairie de Holle (1,480 metres). Continue along the side of the meadow Turn left at La Holle (1,510 metres) and head down through beech woods to the Pont de Saint-Savin

Pont de Saint-Savin
(see map ref 6)
1,436m

Follow the left bank for about 250 metres, then climb straight upwards to the road, which runs from the Ossoue dam to Gavarnie.

Detour, *20 mins*
GAVARNIE
🏠 ⛺ 🚌 ℹ

Take the road mentioned above, to the right, south-east. This is a famous centre for climbing and exploring in the Marboré massif, from the big Cascade du Cirque to the frontier peaks and the Brèche de Roland.

0:30

The GR10 crosses the road and goes up at an angle to a high tension cable. After passing beneath it, you curve round to the right of the hillock called Turoun de Tési.

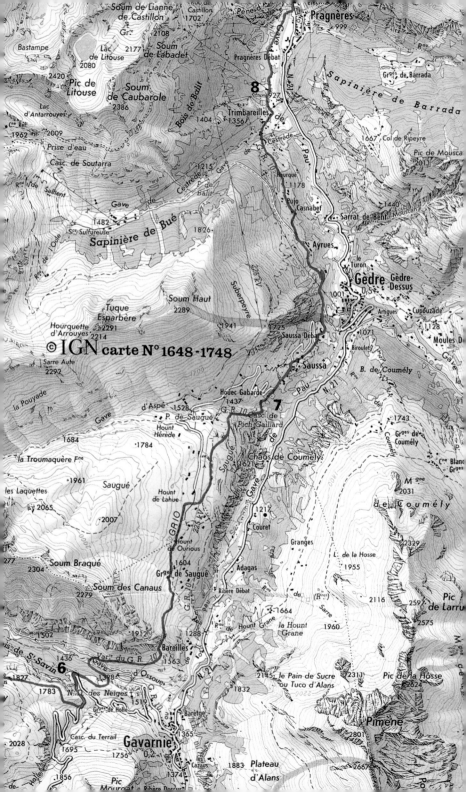

TUROUN DE TÉSI
Ⓐ
1,563m
No water.

0:45

Follow the high-tension cable for about an hour. At first you descend slightly to the north, then you go up for 20 minutes. There are several animal or jeep tracks going off to the right. The occasionally narrow track passes the outlet built for the fountain at Les Canaous and then runs beside a small stream, as the view opens out to the Cirque de Gavarnie to the south. Keep close to the stream until you reach a series of springs, the Hount dets Ourious (red gravel spring), whose waters are channelled into the vast meadows to the north and east. The footpath continues on the level, and then drops down slightly to the right (east) to cross the Chemin du Plateau de Sàugué.

Chemin du Plateau de Sàugué
1,640m
*A track fit for vehicles,
leading, to the north, to
Sàussa and the GR.*

1:0

Continue down to the east, then turn left near a high-tension cable pylon. The track gradually veers away from the cable across grassy hillocks (sites for camping trips), heading north and then north-east. After a rapid descent, first into a rocky valley, then to the right, through clumps of hazel trees, the footpath reaches a rushing mountain stream, and the Gave d'Aspé footbridge.

Footbridge across the
Gave d'Aspé
(see map ref 7)
1,285m
Pich Gaillard waterfall

0:45

Cross the Aspé stream: the bank is crumbling for a few metres and requires care. After passing a year-round spring, there are a few hairpin bends, on the left, leading to the road down to the hamlet of Sàussa. Take the path immediately on the right, which rejoins the road, leaves it again, and joins it yet again before reaching the Débat area. Carry on down to the fork in the Gèdre road.

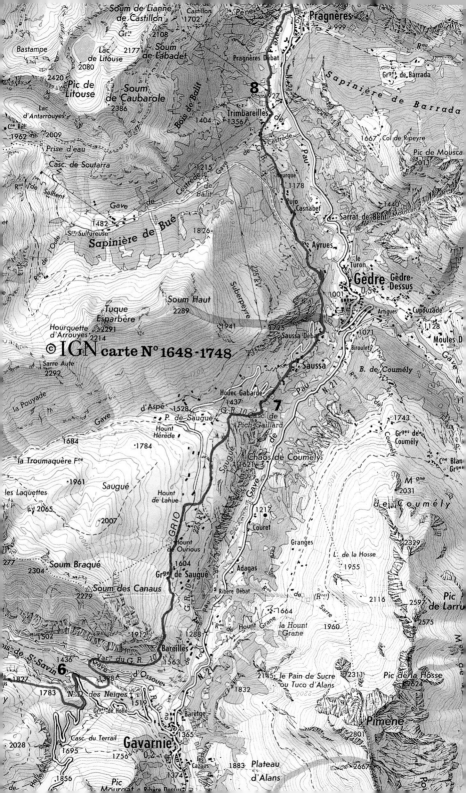

© IGN carte N° 1648-1748

Marmots

Marmots are a thoroughly attractive breed of creature, mountain-dwellers by nature; their very presence confers on somewhat rough scenery a note of humour which is both fantastical and down-to-earth. They are certainly behind the many tales of gnomes, `little people', guardians of buried treasure, which fill the old northern legends; and it must be admitted that their thick fur, which makes them somewhat clumsy, their friendly little faces, comic attitudes, prehensile `hands', and their habit of rearing up on their hind legs to nibble at some particularly succulent delicacy, inspect their surroundings, or give the alert, all are irresistibly reminiscent of miniature humans, simultaneously awkward and lively.

They are usually seen at dawn, as soon as the sun begins to warm the threshold of their undergone dwellings, putting the tips of their noses cautiously outside, advancing and then drawing back, examining the familiar terrain carefully for several minutes, as if this same terrain had made use of the hours of darkness to plot the downfall of all marmots! Finally, if nothing moves and the world is apparently at peace, and their stomachs demand food urgently, they take the plunge and advance jerkily, nibbling their standard breakfast.

This is the moment for long-distance expeditions, taking them at least a hundred metres from their precious hearths; but let a shadow fall on the moraine, or a stone slide down the snowfield, a crow sweep down with shrill cawing, and the little cowards bounce back into their holes like so many jack-in-the-boxes: eating must wait awhile. Samivel, `Cimes et Merveilles' (Arthaud).

Fork in the Gèdre road,
1,080m
Detour, *15 mins,*
GÈDRE
🏠 ⚐ ⚓
1,000m.
Continue down, following the road and its shortcuts.

1:10

Trimbareilles
(see map ref 8)
1,000m

1:0

Turn left on to the road up to Ayruès. There is a good view south-east, over the Héas valley, the Troumouse Cirque, and the frontier col of La Munia. On leaving the hamlet there is a fork. Turn right, on to the road leading to the hamlet of Pujo. Beyond Pujo the footpath passes over a small col and heads down the Burret bridge over the Cestrède stream. Cross this and enter the hamlet of Trimbareilles.

Continue down the road and, at the next hamlet, take the old track. Above the bakery pick up the road again, leaving it a little further on to take the footpath to the left. This gradually narrows as you walk through bushes. Finally you return to the road and cross the Gavarnie stream opposite the Pragnères electricity power station. To the east is the Barrada valley which is famous for its marmot colony.

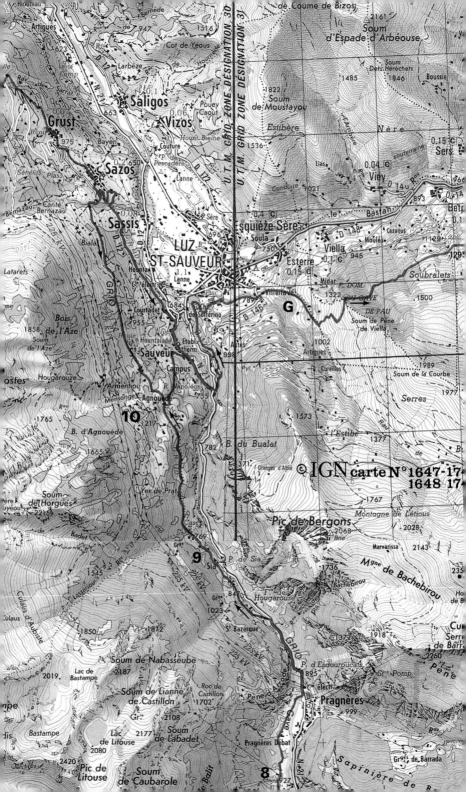

Detour
SAINT-BAZERQUE
🏕 ♈ 🏛

*At the first crossroads
leave the road to take a
drive which leads, within a
few moments, to the Saint-
Bazerque café.*

Croix de Sia
(see map ref 9)
1,025m
*Wooden cross erected at
the highest point of the
path.*

0.45

Saint-Sauveur
(see map ref 10)
738m
*Junction with the GR10
from Cauterets via the Col
de Riou.*

0.40

Bridge of Luz-Saint-Sauveur
720m

After crossing the bridge, face the Pragnères power station and turn left on to the N21, which crosses back over the stream.

After the crossroads, follow the GR to the right above the road, until you reach the hamlet of Sia. Take a paved track leading upwards, then a footpath through the brushwood, to the Sia cross.

Go down through the bushes. There are many different tracks here so you should pay close attention to the waymarking. Cross a road which, to the right, goes down to Saint-Sauveur and, to the left, leads along a level hillside path to the village of Sazos. Here it meets the GR10 alternative route from Cauterets to Luz-Saint-Sauveur via the Col de Riou. Continue through the bushes until you come to the road again. Follow it for a few hundred metres, and then leave it by turning left to cross the Couriol plateau with its well-kept meadows. Follow the fence to the right, then cross over it to enter a plantation of trees. Walk down a steep slope which brings you to a promenade which follows the Riu d'Agnouède to the spa resort of Saint-Sauveur.

Turn right (south-east) on to the N21, which after 5 minutes takes you up to the Napoleon Bridge (755 metres), a bold and elegant structure which, crosses the Pau river gorge, in a single span 80 metres high. On the other side of the bridge cross the Luz-Gavarnie road and take the Astés footpath, leaving it to the right at the second hairpin bend. The walking here is undemanding: houses, springs, shade, then a well-kept area round the chapel known as Solférino (about 760 metres). Beside it is an obelisk: this is a Napoleonic souvenir, one of many in the valley. The route heads downwards, following the cementery road and then upwards along the Ise stream. On your left is the Luz-Saint-Sauveur bridge.

Continue along the Ise to the hamlet of Villenave (see map ref G). Cross the bridge (789 metres) and continue across the hillside, first heading north-east, and then, for a much greater distance, to the south-east. When you come to the footpath, climb

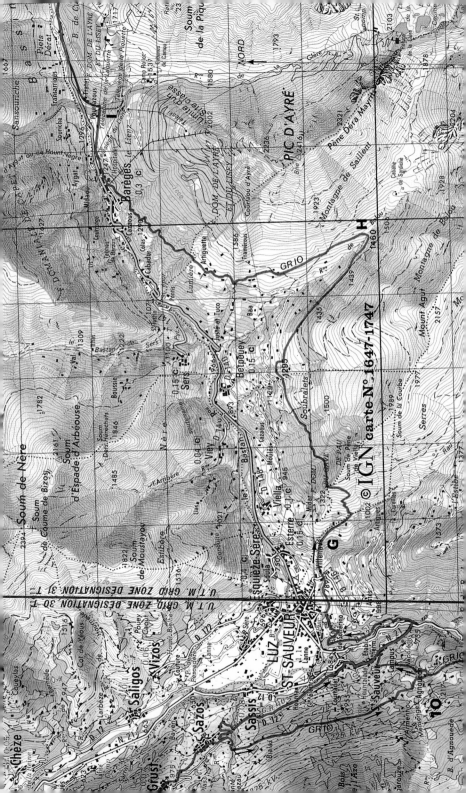

Detour, 3 min
LUZ-SAINT-SAUVEUR
⌂ ⌂ Ӽ ⚒ ﷽

*Old town; centre for
exploration of the many
surrounding villages with
their beautiful old houses,
ancient alleyways and
Norman churches.
Hospitallers' church
fortified in 14th century;
Norman church at Sère;
Chateau of Sainte-Marie.*

1:30

few metres up the slope to an irrigation channel.

Irrigation channel,
1090m

1:0

Cross this to the right, and go up through the grasslands. Carry on to the left, along an ash hedge, to the Couret crest, where there is an extensive view to the north. Pass a barn (1,133 metres) and then leave the crest to ford a spring which flows all year round. Now follow the route as it climbs up heathery slopes in wide bends, which are steep enough to demand care when the ground is wet. Finally, bear left on a level with the Couret d'Ousset.

Couret d'Ousset
1,322m

0:40

This pass is marked by a dressed stone on the right, and on the left by a flat salt stone and a shady ledge with boulders and pine trees. This is the entrance to the Ousset wood, or the Viella estate forest (see IGN map ref, the Gave de Pau), a beautiful pinewood designed to conserve the soil, which used to wash down into the villages and farm buildings. The GR10 heads down in short hairpin bends, rises a little, then remains virtually level, often broad, always clear. The forest gives way to increasingly sparse clumps of trees above enormous grassy slopes dotted with small farms. The path leads down to an old canal, and follows it to a crossroads (1,295m).

Crossroads
Detour, *15 mins,*
LE BOLOU GITE
⌂

1:20

*1,300m.
Carry on along the old
canal, east-south-east, for
about 10 minutes, then
descend to the road. The
bridge over the river is*

Continue walking steadily up and along, then follow another canal, and climb up still further to a level stretch and the ford at Bolou.

111

©IGN carte N°1747

*below the barn-gite of
Bolou on the right bank.*

Gué (Ford) at Le Bolou
(see map ref H)
1,460m
*If the current appears too
strong, the river can be
crossed a little way above
the marked route*

Cross the river and continue along the other bank to the north, again following a canal. Soon you can look down on the pleasant, flatter areas of the Pla dets Plaas, followed by La Lumière and l'Artiguète; camping is allowed here once the hay is cut. The track through the grass grows gradually narrower, until it reaches a fork marked with two ONF signposts. A 200 metre loop left and right leads to a broad horizontal track, below a barn.

1:10   **Detour,** *15 mins*
LE BOLOU GITE
(see page 109)
*Go down to the farm road
close by. This runs below
the barn-gite, which lies
upstream from the river
bridge.*

About 250 metres from the barn, go down into a ravine. You swiftly come to a good track; turn right along it, into the Ayré Estate Forest.

Ayré Estate Forest
*(see IGN map, Gave de
Pau).*
*The centuries old trees
provide protection from the
landslips which formerly
devastated the valley.*

The footpath becomes a track leading down to Barèges.

BARÈGES
(see map ref I)
1,240m

Without going into the town centre, the GR10 passes the Hospitalet, and after a few metres, takes two bends down to the left, then up again along the Duc du Maine lane, which turns into a footpath beneath the cable-car lines. When you leave the Culousque wood, take the N618, then turn left on to the station road. Leave this at the bridge over the Dets Coubous River, and go up the right bank. Cross the N618 slightly to the east of La Gaubie Bridge.

1:15

PONT DE LA GAUBIE
(see map ref J)
1,538m

Follow the well marked footpath up to the south until it meets a track suitable for vehicles, which you can see above you. Follow this road for about 1,500 metres. Shortly beyond a small bridge (see IGN map ref Pountou) you come to the fork of the Dets Coubous lake.

0:40

113

©IGN carte N°1747 1748

2:0

1:20

1:0

Fork of the
Lac dets Coubous
1,750m

CABANE D'AYGUES-
CLUSES
⌂
2,150m

Col de Madamète
(see map ref K)
2,509m
Views of beautiful snowy
slopes and, in the far
distance, the massif of
Mount Perdu, in Spain

The Néouvielle Nature
Reserve
This nature reserve lies in
the high valley of the Nest
d'Aure, some 30 kilometres
from Lourdes, between the
peak of Le Midi de Bigorre
and the Spanish frontier. It
ranges from 1,800 metres
to 3,091 metres high,
containing forests, grassy
meadows studded with
frequent lakes, some
permanent snow-fields,
and rocky mountain peaks.

Detour, *45 mins*
CHALET D'ORÉDON
⌂
1,856m.
Take the D177 road.

Take the footpath on the left heading up the valley of Aygues Cluses (underground waters). The valley is narrow at first, then broadens out through a series of hollows, which are marshy to varying degrees. Keep to the edges, walking through pines, which cease shortly before the Cabane d'Aygues-Cluses.

Climb to the south, then the south-west, passing between the Madamète lakes (see map ref K). Follow the rather scanty traces of the path across the scree. After the last, unnamed, lake at 2,469 metres, you reach the Col de Madamète.

At this point, the path enters the Néouvielle National Nature Reserve. Go down into the valley, along the right bank of the river. Before you come to the little lake at 2,398 metres, called Le Gourg de Rabas, cross to the left bank and continue on down through big blocks of granite and then, further down, ancient pine trees, which are very rare in France, at a height of 2,500 metres. You come out on grassy shoulders within sight of the Aumar lake, one of the most attractive in the Pyrénées.

The GR10 follows the western shore of Lake Aumar. Ford the natural outlet and, beyond an uninhabited house, you come to the culvert of the EDF (Electricité de France) spillway and the Route des Lacs.

Alternative route from Lake Aumar to Col d'Estoudou, known as the `Route des Lacs' (see map ref L). You start at an altitude of 2,192 metres and, after visiting the chalet, return to the GR10 by taking shortcuts for about 10 minutes up to D177 (1,912 metres). Bear right (east), along a small dry ravine and then, as the trees grow thicker, continue up a fairly steep valley. On the way out of the forest there is a spring in the pastures. Carry on in the same direction (east), until you meet the GR10 just below the Col d'Estoudou.

Beyond the culvert the GR10 heads east along the narrow grassy strip between the road and the lake, and then continues, still heading east, across hummocky pasture land. The track through the Passades d'Aumar

115

1:20

Col d'Estoudou
2,260m.
40 minutes to
the left (north)
at Monpelat is a
viewpoint over the
lake region

1:0

LAC DE L'OULE
⌂
(see map ref M)
1,821m

1:15

Fork at
LE BASTAN
⌂
(see map ref N)
2,110m.
Junction of GR10c

0:30

forest is easy to follow. Continue on down to the Ermite fountain, a spring at 2,130 metres, for the start of the climb to the Col d'Estoudou.

Descend to the east across the grasslands and through the Lude fir woods. The track winds through the trees, crosses a clearing, and reaches Lake de l'Oule.

The next stretch of the GR10 crosses a fairly isolated area, with vast horizons, where walking is difficult in bad weather. `Escape routes' are marked. The first is the track beside the lake. If you follow this to the right, after 30 minutes, you reach the tarmac road down the Aure Valley.

At the Lake d'Oule, the GR10 sets off to the left (north), past an old stone hut. Beyond the bridge and behind the Lude hut, which has two basic shelters, the path turns left up a steep slope, then right on to a broad drovers' track across slopes, studded with old pine trees. At the edge of the trees, before reaching an isolated rock and a spring, turn to the left on to a footpath, just as it bends, heading up to the north above the trees. A small col opens out to a view over the upper Bastan valley. Pass the Bastan hut with its shepherd, leaving it on the left, to reach the Bastan fork.

Alternative route (GR10c) - Le Bastan to Artigues-de-Gripp. This detour connects the Néouville region of the GR10 to the Valley of the Adour and the RN618 (Route des Pyrénées). The route runs entirely along mountain footpaths above 1,200 metres, on both sides of the Col de Bastanet. It crosses a region of lakes and forests scattered with open grassy areas, where rural activities take place.. Snow persists for six months of the year. There is a modern refuge on each slope.

Above the shepherd's hut at Le Bastan the route climbs to the north. After a short while, you walk along the right shore of the very pretty Lac Inferieur (2,141 metres), the first in the series of Bastanet lakes . To the left is Le

Laquet summit (2,197 metres) then the Lac du Milieu, which is dominated to the east by a wooded saddle. 30 minutes after leaving the hut at Le Bastan you reach the Refuge de Bastanet.

REFUGE DE BASTANET
⌂
2,240m
Also known as the
PTT Refuge.

Climb gently up to the Lac Superieur (2,260 metres) then across the last grassland which is suitable for camping. After crossing the outflow via a ford, you wind through big rocks on the edge of the scree zone. Cross this to reach the wild, natural amphitheatre of Bastan. Dominant on the right is Le Pichaley, which is separated from the Pic de Bastan by the col of the same name. The ridge slopes away very slightly to the left until the Pic de Portarras, which is itself separated from the Pic de Batan by the easily distinguishable Col de Bastanet. The large clumps of pine trees reach an altitude of 2,400 metres, while the path climbs, sometimes very steeply, across loose stones and rocks, to reach the Bastanet Col or `horquette' at 2,507 metres. From here, you descends very rapidly over rocky or grassy saddles, where the rather indistinct track requires some care. It becomes clearer by the Hourquette Lakes (2,405 metres), and winds between then, leaving only the largest to the left (see left).

1:45

Also on the left is the wide footpath to the Hourquette de Caderolles. Walkers coming from the other direction may be tempted to take this by mistake. The gentle slope takes you between a pair of twin lakes, them more abruptly to the Campana Refuge.

REFUGE DE CAMPANA
⌂
2,225m

The route descends swiftly, still heading north, to the ford at the Grésiolles reservoir of the EDF. Walk along its right bank, first at the high-water mark (2,115 metres) and then higher up on the saddle, coming down again to the foot of the barrage, amid the depressing and all-too-visible remains of EDF works. Continue to the reservoir of the small lakes and walk beside it, to the left, for a long way. Eventually, you pass between the retaining wall and the EDF building.

1:0

Retaining wall and EDF building
2,041m.

Go swiftly down through steep pasture land, with a line of wooden posts across it. The path follows these fairly closely for several kilometres.

0:45

Fork
1,680m.

1:15

ARTIGUES-DE-GRIPP
🏠 △ ✕ ⊞
1,200m.
Small holiday resort at foot
of the Pic du Midi de
Bigorre, with a deservedly
famous panorama and
observatory.

These enormous pastures are twice interrupted by the escarpments of Les Passets where the rocky surface, if wet, needs care. Immediately after the second there is a fork.

A footpath leads straight to a hairpin bend on the D618 road, but the route turns right and descends rapidly, picking up the line of posts again, and crossing the Garet mountain river on a footbridge with a barrier to prevent flocks from using it. Shortly afterwards, you come to the Milomés spring, which is controlled, and has a reputation for drying up only once every eighty years! The path soon crosses a very large, level grassy area, the Pla de Garet. To the north, there is a spring and short-stay camp site. At the next small col (1,559 metres) a footpath goes off to the left. Follow this down to the D618, the Baregès-Artigues-Campan road. The clearly marked GR carries on down obliquely across slopes, which are sometimes slippery, passing the Hounts de la Yègue (La Jument springs), Margalit, a tiny but perennial cool stream, and La Béziaou. You pass close to the Garet River as it falls in a fine cascade, within sight of the village. The swift descent follows the waterfall along the steep, wooded bank, where it is dangerous to veer to the left. Cross a precarious footbridge, which can be avoided by going to the right across the unloading yard. On the left bank the path crosses a grassy flat area to the edge of the hamlet of Artigues-de-Gripp.

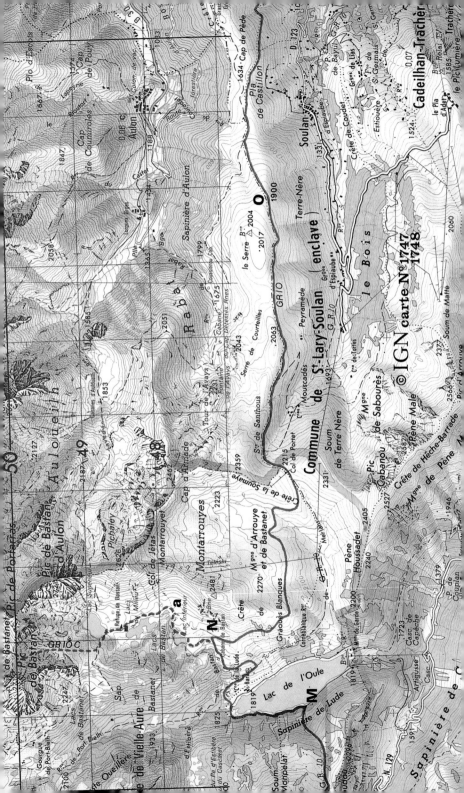

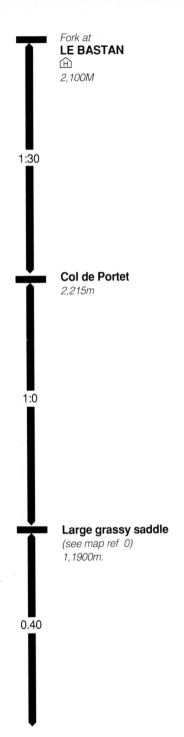

Fork at
LE BASTAN
⌂
2,100M

1:30

Col de Portet
2,215m

1:0

Large grassy saddle
(see map ref 0)
1,1900m.

0.40

To continue on the GR10 turn right (southwards) and follow the route as it rises gently to cross the ever-steeper slopes 300 metres above the Lake d'Oule. The drovers' road with its multiple tracks should be negotiated with care if the ground is damp when it crosses a small rocky ravine. After half an hour, as you walk along a long bend to the left (east) over the Corneblanque rocky outcrop, the slopes become very gentle. The footpath across the vast Arrouye grasslands is more or less level, and crosses several ski-lift lines. It then veers gradually to the right (south) fords two streams, and climbs on to a saddle, with a road running round it. The footpath joins the road and comes to a hut before reaching the Col de Portet.

The road continues through the col, which can be useful when visibility is poor, and goes down to the village of Soulan, (2 hours), before crossing the GR10 twice above Vielle-Aure. However, the GR10 leaves the road to the right to take the old drovers' track, which after a few moments reaches the Santhous spring. From here you descend to the east for quite a long time, keeping steadily to the right (south) of the ridge. Frequently very clearly marked, the route descends steadily, nearly joins the road again, then becomes less clear over the level grassland. However, it becomes clearer again later and reaches a col, (1,965 metres), from where you can see the broad plain to your left. The track is then very clear as it crosses the sloping grassland to a large grassy saddle.

The track is not very clear and the drovers' road has several branches. The best path is across the middle of the saddle, marked on the open ground by wooden stakes, which you should use a guide. The slope becomes steeper and the view opens out over the Aure valley and, on the left, the Arbizon massif. Still on the saddle, at about 1,700 metres, a broad footpath joins the GR10 on the left. Once again, the pathway becomes less distinct as it crosses successive level stretches, which should be left slightly to the right. Bear to the right to cross the lowest level stretch, called the Pla de Castillon.

© IGN carte N°1747-1847
1748-1848

Pla de Castillon
1,606m
AULON
Detour, *1hr.*
⌂

Follow the yellow and red markings heading northwards indicating the Tour de la Vallée d'Aure.

2:0

VIELLE-AURE
⌂⌂✕ ⚅
(see map ref P)
800m

0:15

Bourisp
800m
Church with Norman belltower and 16th century frescoes.

1:15

AZET
⌂⌂✕
(see map ref Q)
1,168m
Historic buildings round the church; fortified house whose tower serves as a belfry.

1:30

Descend obliquely to the right keeping to the same ridge. The footpath goes firmly downhill, leaving more horizontal tracks to each side. The Neste d'Aure river is spread out in the valley, and on the opposite slopes you can see villages which the GR10 passes through later. Beyond a ford turn right on to a paved track. Then leave it at the first hairpin bend by turning left, on the level, into a steep meadow above the Pladérès barns. A little further on you walk through clumps of hazel bushes and then pastureland where you descend slightly. A sharp right bend, with the last of the marker posts, brings you back to hazel bushes. From here, the footpath goes steeply down in numerous hairpin bends. Cross the road twice. This is the road which walkers can take up the hill, when mist makes walking uncertain on the ridge. Cross a ford and follow the road into Vielle-Aure.

The GR10 crosses the Neste d'Aure, a mountain river with clear waters, much favoured for fishing and water sports. Beyond the bridge turn left, and then right along the first track. Cross the N129 and, 200 metres further on, you come to the village of Bourisp.

Above the village, to the south, a good track climbs up above the deep Mousquère ravine, which lies to your right. Go through the village of Estensan. As you leave the village, pass the D255 road to the left, and continue on the narrow tarmac track to the hamlet of Autur, and then take a narrow footpath bordered with ash trees to the village of Azet.

Go round the church and up the Louron Road between Azet and Adervielle. Leave it after 300 metres to turn right on to a broad footpath which climbs steeply upwards. Heading southeast, cross long grassy slopes, with scattered ash trees and barns. The route takes you close by some of them. At an altitude of about 1,435 metres cross the road. The route soon becomes narrow, passing some fine old drinking troughs above the last barn, and then splitting up as it crosses the grassland. Keep to the right, above the road, for about 15 minutes. After a muddy stretch by a spring, where the road heads off to the south, keep

© IGN carte N°1848

climbing to the east-south-east to reach the Couret de Latuhe, which is close at hand.

Couret de Latuhe
(see map ref R)
1,586m.
Detour, 1hr 20mins
**GITE D'ADERVIELLE
DES AMIS DE LA
NATURE**
⌂

Follow a footpath, which may have painted markings, and goes off horizontally to the left. You soon walk down to the farm building enclosures at Nabias. Continue straight through the woods to the village of Aderville and the Saint-Éloi chapel. From here, go down towards the Neste until you reach the gite. From here it is possible to return to the GR10 at Loudenvielle, 2.5 kilometres away, by following the road.

From Couret de Latuhe, the GR10 crosses a dirt track, keeping to the saddle on the right. Cross the Azet-Loudenvielle road, and then the road which, to the right, leads in 10 minutes to the resort of Val Louron. Roadworks may affect the terrain for the next kilometre. Beyond a level stretch, where the path crosses another dirt track, walk to the right of an isolated rocky outcrop, drop down for 200 metres through heathland, and then turn left on to the drovers' road which leads to the wall of the Granges de Paulède enclosure.

0:30

Granges de Paulède
enclosure
About 1,380m

Once again cross a dirt track on the right, keeping the wall with its row of large ash trees on your left. The route descends rapidly, crosses a ford and reaches a bridge. Cross this and follow a wide track. After 400 metres, turn right on to the grassy footpath, which overlooks the villages and the lake of Le Louron. Go down long hairpin bends until you meet, on the right, a winding footpath which opens out on to grassland and shrubs and reaches a stream on the right which has to be forded four times. Continuing first through trees, and then through attractive wooded scenery the path becomes broader, passes a camp site, and then takes the Pont du Prat over the Neste du Louron into the village of Loudenvielle.

0:50

Loudenvielle
970m.
The Louron valley has many places to visit; almost all the tiny villages have Norman churches, and many have ancient

Alternative route from Loudenvielle to the Ourtiga hut (2.5hrs). In the spring, this route is preferable to the GR10. From Loudenvielle go south on the D25 for 500 metres. Beyond the bridge (975 metres) turn right on to a cart track, which is lined with big trees and leads to the power station. This path crosses the

frescoes. Climbs up towards the Spanish frontier lead to the lonely high valleys of Caillaouas, Pouchergues, Aygues Tortes, and La Pez.

road twice and climbs up to the right through farm buildings near The Neste for 500 metres. It then bears left (east) and crosses the road on the right at the Pont des Chèvres (1,103 metres).

PONT DE CHEVRES
⌂
2:30

Take the broad track going up the left bank of the river Aube; the track soon becomes narrow, and reaches the Pont de Hournets (1,266 metres). Here it is joined by a track coming from Germ (see left) along the right bank of the river. Continues up the track through the Aoubère fir trees to the IGN map ref 1487. At this point, on the other (right) bank the GR10 comes in from Germ. Continue along the left bank to the Ourtiga hut.

OURTIGA HUT
⌂
(see map ref S)
1,620m

1:10

Come down slightly here in order to cross the mountain stream at the ford, then rejoin the GR10 on the other side of the stream. If the river is in flood, go down to the riverside to the south-east of the hut: the ford is not easy to cross in times of flood, and you should go far round to the right and ford the four successive tributary streams. After the final one, which is never very big, pick up the waymarkings again.

The GR10 leaves Loudenvielle heading east: at a crossroads before reaching the church square, take a track which turns into a footpath. This climbs and winds through pastureland and copses to the village of Germ.

GERM
⌂
1,339m
In the church, there is a statue of the Virgin, typical of Pyrenean art.

1:30

Take the tarmac road southwards out of the village, for about 200 metres. Leaving it to the right, turn on to a footpath, which climbs up beside a stream and then crosses it. Carry on south and then south-west beside a low drystone wall, across a grassy shoulder and pasture land. The footpath continues on the level across very large slopes, with fine views over the Louron valley and the summits of the central chain of mountains. After a while, the slopes become steeper. Cross a steep avalanche corridor, where there is snow or scree. Cross with great care if the annual path-clearing has not been done, and above all, if the ground is wet. Alternatively, descend to the grasslands near the track coming from

© IGN carte N°1848

Germ. Turn left (south) on this, to the Hournets bridge and pick up the alternative route described earlier.

You reach the stream again at an altitude of about 1,487 metres; on the other side is the alternative route coming from Loudenvielle via the Pont des Chèvres and the Pont de Hournets. Remain on the right bank, and climb up to a large shoulder.

Large shoulder
(see map ref S)
1,600m.

On a level with the Ourtiga hut, on the other side of the stream, the GR10 follows the course of a small stream, crossing it a little further on. Go up between two ravines, following a path which is not very clear, to a grassy saddle. Then climb, bearing left, to the foot of the rocky escarpment. The track becomes almost horizontal and crosses a river bed which is frequently dry. Head towards a col along a grassy coomb, which becomes gradually narrower. The going is easy as far as the Pas de Couret.

1:40

Pas de Couret
2,131m.
This col is not
indicated
on the IGN 1:50,000
map.

Detour, *3 hrs*
Les Agudes
(Ski resort)
Follow a high altitude
footpath to the N618 at the
Col de Peyresourde, or to
either of the ski resorts of
Les Agudes and Germ

2:15

Detour
Espingo refuge
To the right, on the south
slopes of the col, are the
markings of a route leading
to the Espingo refuge. This
route is extremely difficult,
and walkers are very
strongly advised not to take
it.

Follow a track down the east slope of the Pas de Couret, then take a footpath leading across scree and pasture land. Follow the Esquierry valley along a stream, passing two shepherd's huts on the right bank. This valley is famous for its wild flowers. At about 1,600 metres go into woodland; a footpath leads through it along numerous hairpin bends to the Val d'Astau. Cross the Neste d'Oô via the Astau bridge, then turn right and follow the road to the Granges d'Astau.

© IGN carte N°1848

GRANGES D'ASTAU
⌂
1:15 *(see map ref I)*
1,139m

Go up the Neste d'Oô on a mule track with frequent hairpin bends, which brings you to the Oô Lake.

LAC D'OÔ
⌂
1:30 *1,504m.*
Fine waterfall.

Keep to the east shore of the Oô Lake following a good footpath. Halfway round the lake, the path goes up to the Col d'Espingo.

Col d'Espingo
(Not marked on the IGN 1:50,000 map)
1,910m

Detour, *5 mins.*
ESPINGO REFUGE
⌂
1.15 *1,967m*
Bear south. Warden from Whitsun — end of September, also at Easter. One room always open.

Turn sharp left and climb north-east to the Hourquette des Hounts-Secs.

Hourquette des Hounts-Secs
1:15 *2,275m*

The footpath climbs and descends, cutting across valleys beneath the north face of the Coume Nère and the Subscale peaks, and reaches the Col de la Coume de Bourg.

Col de la Coume de Bourg
(see map ref U)
2,272m

Detour, *30 mins.*
Pic de Céciré
1:30 *2,403 metres.*
Head north-east on a footpath leading up to this magnificent viewpoint overlooking the whole region.

Follow the route to the left (north-east) on the Pic de Céciré footpath. Then bear east on a footpath, which passes a spring and a ruined hut to the right and then gently descends along the southern slopes of the Pic de Céciré. Follow a ridge to the plateau of Superbagnères, at 1,831 metres. From there descend to the Hotel de Superbagnères.

HOTEL DE SUPERBAGNÉRES
⌂
2:30 *1,804m.*
Winter and summer sports resort.

On reaching the road from Luchon to Superbagnéres, in front of the big hotel, turn left on to the old bobsleigh track, which heads first south-west and then north. After six hairpin bends it comes to the old Artigues Ardoune stop, which can provide basic shelter. Continue downwards along many hairpin bends, heading north. To your left, you pass the Pales du Mail spring. Enter Luchon on the Superbagnères track, near the market.

BAGNÈRES-DE-LUCHON

🏠 ⌂ ⚑ 🚂 🚌

(see map ref V)
650m
Thermal springs

3:0

ARTIGUE

⌂

(see map ref W)
1,230m

1:30

Cabane de Saunères
1,660m.
Fine view over the chain of
mountain peaks;
water 8 minutes away
to east.

1.0

PLAN DE MONTMAJOU

⌂

(see map ref X)
1,930m
The frontier with Spain is
marked out on the nearest
ridge.

To cross Luchon, take the Superbagnères track, then the Rue Laity, Avenue Jean-Jaurès, Rue du Docteur Germès, Place Joffre, Place du Comminges, Avenue Maréchal Foch and Avenue de Toulouse. Turn right, go under the railway bridge, and then immediately turn left, following the road as far as Juzet-de-Luchon. As you come out of Juzet, turn right on to a footpath which crosses the D46 five times and then joins it for 500 metres outside Sode. In Sode turn left, near the bottom of the village, on to the Salles track, which is marked no 13. Follow this along the side of the hill through the Pau woods. Cross a ravine and continue along the hillside again, then up along hairpin bends to the village of Artigue.

Behind the church, take a broad track leading to the north-east until you reach a stream. Bear right beside it for about 200 metres before crossing it. The footpath goes up to the north, without going into the wood. It turns sharply to the right and curves round to the edge of the Auédau wood. Here it veers right (south) again, then via two hairpin bends climbs up to the Cabane de Saunères.

Turn left, heading north-east. Pass a tall pine tree which has been blown down by storms. However, this may now have been cut up and removed. The footpath crosses the rocky crest of Créspés and, on the north slope, winds through the Cigalères rocks to come out at the Plan de Montmajou.

Take a footpath north, to the left, between the frontier ridge on the right and the Auédau wood on the left. The path soon comes to a drinking trough.

Alternative route from the drinking trough to the Cigalères crest. From the trough take the footpath furthest to the left, (north-west) leading down across grassland and heather almost to IGN map ref 1835. At a shepherd's hut, take the old miners' track up to the north-east across the rocky Mail de l'Aigle ridge. After a while you will have to ford several small streams, tributaries of the river Sarrouègère. Next, the footpath bears right above the Dessous pool. Pass a shepherd's hut and, 250 metres further on after the path has

©IGN carte N°1847
1848

2:0

Cigalères Ridge
2,093m

changed direction, pass the Dessous pool (2,018 metres). Climb up, heading due north, to the Cigalères crest (2,093 metres).

This route should only be followed in fine weather. Beyond the drinking trough, follow a footpath going downwards, for about 200 metres. Then climb up again to the right to the col of Les Taons de Bacanère (1,976 metres) where there are the posts of a cable railway and a ruined hut. This col is on the frontier ridge. Follow the crest to the north-east, along the boundary markers numbered from 398 to 404. The GR10 goes slightly below the Bacanère summit (2,193 metres) on the west side, passing boundary marker no 405. Continue along the west slope of La Hage summit, where you join up with the alternative route on the Cigalères ridge.

Cross this ridge at the Col d'Esclot d'Aou, which is not marked on the IGN 1:50,000 map, between the Burat and La Hage summits.

Ossoue Valley, towards Gavannie, from Petit Vignemale above Hourquette d'Ossoue.

© IGN carte N°1847-1947
1848-1948

Follow the route through a gate set on a chicane, and descend steeply to the north. A ittle further on turn right (east) towards Saint-Béat pool (1,891 metres). Pass to the left of it. Go down to the left (north) on the slopes of the Burat peak. The path bears to the right by a spring and leads on to the south slopes of the Palarguère peak. Shortly afterwards, you come to the Corraus huts.

1:0

CABANES DES COURRAUS
⌂
(see map ref Y)
1,586m

Descend to the south-east and enter the wood. Soon, at a clearing, the path comes to the Artigue hut (see left).

ARTIGUE HUT

2:30

Go back into the wood, heading north. Cross a stream and follow it downstream at a short distance from the back. The slope becomes steeper and the stream cascades down; the path continues downwards into the Batch valley. At 1,110 metres turn off a steep haulage track to take a footpath to the left, (north-north-west). Cross a stream and you come out to the Artiguessans hut, 1025 metres. Turn sharp right (south) to the Batch stream, and cross it. Now follow it downstream. Cross it four times, and at the last bridge, nearly at the edge of the wood, turn right. About 1 kilometre further on, the footpath goes up to the right in the wood. However, you continue along the edge of the wood to a track. Turn left and walk along it to the N125 (formerly the N618) beside a calvary. Turn right on to the N125 road and head towards Fos.

FOS
Ⓗ ⌂ 🚟 🚌
544m

WALK 3

Melles
719m
Detour, *1 hour.*
FOS
🏠 ⌂ ⚒
544m
Fos is reached via the D44 and N125 roads.

Labach de Melles
980m

1:30

CABANE D'ULS
⌂
1,868m
Situated in the middle of marshy region.

2:30

Pas du Bouc
2,170m
Here you can see the Etang d'Uls down below.

0:20

Leave the village via the D44, which runs above the Maudun stream to the hamlet of Labach de Melles.

Here the tarmac road ends and the GR10 follows the footpath which goes upstream, on the left-hand side of the Maudun valley. You cross a stream, the Séridède, and, first passing a fork to your left leading to the old mines of Blende de Pale Bidau, you cross the stream of La Goute de Peyre-Nère. The path enters a beech forest and rises swiftly to the Auède waterfall. Cross the river and continue upstream along the right bank. At the beginning of season it is not unusual to meet with hardened snow here, the residue of former avalanches. The GR10 crosses the wetter, north-facing side of the valley and just before it enters a pine forest, you will come across the Salières spring on your right. You cross over two channels scoured by avalanches, where the snow usually remains until late into the season, and then emerge from the forest. The path, known locally as Les Anglès, twists and turns before crossing a stream and reaching the Uls shelter.

You climb a gentle slope and, walking in a south-easterly direction, cross the Uls pastures. You should be able to see old mineworkings about 300 metres away to your right. The track is initially easy to make out, but along the flank of the Canau Grande it begins to blend into the grass. It becomes clearer again just before the Pas du Bouc.

Follow an almost level path south-east for an easy walk to the Auéran pass.

© IGN carte N° 1947
1948

Col d'Auéran
2,176m
Detour
1.5 hrs.
The Crabère peak is easily scaled from this point.

0:30

You leave the pass down its eastern slope, overlooking the Etang d'Araing, and head for the Etang d'Araing shelter.

ETANG D'ARAING
⌂
(see map ref A)
1,950m
Detour
The route markers here to the Tour de Biros

0:45

The path leads you below the dam and in front of the lakeside shelter, climbing south-east over bare grazing land and roughly following a high tension cable on your right. The track occasionally gets lost in amongst the stony terrain, so keep the cable in sight as a route marker. As you climb to the top of the pasture and, with the electric pylon 150 metres up on your left, you are walking on the Serre d'Araing.

Serre d'Araing
2,221m.
Fine views over the Couserans mountains.

0:45

The path keeps to the left of the electric cable, never more than 150 metres away from it, then drops rapidly and runs along the edge of a cliff. From here you can see the Etang de Chichoué, which used to provide the power for the mines of Bentaillou. The GR10 continues to descend, passing three white marker stones and a tombstone before arriving at the Bentaillou mines.

MINEWORKINGS OF BENTAILLOU
⌂
1,870m.
Mine used to produce lead and zinc. Do not venture into the tunnels, there is a danger of collapse.

0:30

The GR10 bears north from the mine, passing below a hut, which can serve as a shelter, and then heading its way eastward. You pass the Cigalère grotto and descend over grassy terrain towards the Catauère pass.

Col de la Catauère
1,076m

0:35

You leave the pass in a southerly direction and follow the pylons that carry the cables and tipper trucks of the old mineworkings. The path meanders on to the Station de Rouge.

Station de Rouge
1,550m.
Do not venture into the mineworks.

1:15

You leave the mining post by a steeply sloping and very winding track. Pass through a beech forest and on the other side you reach the village of Eylie.

144

EYLIE D'EN HAUT

⌂

990m

0:15

The path passes the partially ruined Bocard factory, which formerly dealt with the crushing and washing of the ore, and enters a dark, damp gorge through which the River Lez runs.

Lez

960m

Detour, *1.5 hrs*

SENTEIN

🏠 ⛺ 🚂 🚌

Go north, first along a track and then to follow the road for 6km

2:45

When in spate, the Lez is more easily negotiated further downstream via a culvert in the middle of the factory. You then follow the track south to link up with the GR. The GR crosses the river via a temporary footbridge and cuts across the track that leads to the factory. You leave the Lez valley in an easterly direction, along the track leading to the Bulard mines which are still in use, on the Spanish side of the frontier: the path overlooks the Lez valley and you should be able to see across to the hydro-electric station at Eylie. You ford the Mont Ner stream (1,180 metres) and then enter the Laspe woods. The track meanders up through the woods and then crosses the summer pastures on the northern flank of the Mail du Bulard massif. You skirt, to the south, the rig that was used to draw up the skips from the Spanish Mines and, passing a ruined shed beneath the Mont Ner ridge, you climb up to the Arech pass.

Col de l'Arech

1,802m.

Panoramic view back towards Serre d'Araing.

0:15

Walk south-east, descending over rocky terrain to the Arech shelter.

CABANE PASTORALE DE L'ARECH

⌂

1,638m

Spring just to the south of the hut.

0:10

Follow the forest track east until you reach a junction.

Junction

1,580m

Junction with footpath linking Cassaings pass with Tour de Biros.

0:45

At this point the route leaves the forest track, which continues on due north, to follow a trail east along the very steep mountain slope flanking the Arech stream until it reaches the edge of a forest. The path levels out and veers right across a ravine, at an altitude of 1,312 metres. Enter the forest and continue south-east to the Arnaca ridge.

Crete d'Arnaca
1,242m.
Old mineworks.

0:20

Descend along the ridge north-north-east for a short distance before turning south into the head of the Orle valley. After a while you come to the footbridge at Grauillès.

GRAUILLÈS FOOTBRIDGE
⌂
1,801m

0:15

The GR10 crosses the footbridge and follows the right bank of the Orle downstream to the ruined hamlet of Flouquet.

Flouquet
1,050m

Alternative route Flouquet to Orle valley (unmarked) 1hr 20 mins. Without losing height you rejoin the GR10 after 1hr 20 mines, on the right bank of the Orle valley, at an altitude of 1,250 metres. The second half of this route makes use of an old mine railway from Porte d'Orle. You will have to negotiate two tunnels where a torch is useful, if not essential. The 1.6 metre height of these tunnels may prove difficult for heavily laden walkers.

1:30

Continue downstream into the neck of the valley for a further 300metres before crossing the mouth of the stream. Almost immediately after, take the Besset woods path. Climb a tightly winding path out on to the right-hand slope of a ravine and then cross the Besset wood. Soon after you enter the wood, you cross over the old railway line, although it is fairly well concealed, at which point you meet the alternative GR route. At an altitude of about 1,400 metres, the path leads across pasture, where it tends to become obscured, and works its way towards the Besset shelter.

CABANE DE BESSET
⌂
1,494m.
Also known as the Bout de la Forêt; shelter providing room for 5 people; a fire can be lit; water 300 metres to the south along the level track.

1:10

Climb first to the south-east up the slope towards a rocky headland, then north and north-east towards a line of rocks. Then turn south-east, crossing some grass and reaching a cabin.

CLOT DU LAC
⌂
1,821m.
This cabin is still used by herdsmen.

0:40

Continue south-east for 1 kilometre following the winding path down over the chain that forms the northern wall of the great Trapech ravine. At the high approach to the ravine, at an altitude of 1,650 metres, the GR turns north-north-east breaking away from the track

and joining another that leads down into the huge, deep valley. This is very good country for summer grazing and several herdsmen's huts are spread across the mountainside. Cross the valley to reach the shelter.

CABANE DU TRAPECH DU MILIEU
⌂

(see map ref C)
Shelter for 6 people; fires can be lit and there is a spring

1:30

Leave the shelter and walk along a twisting path, which leads to the Artigue hut. Cross the stream and, bypassing a landslide, go down the left bank as far as another hut, which is closed to walkers, where you take the path that links up with the forest road. When you come to a grassy area called the Pla de la Lau ,follow the road over the bridge, which brings you to a shelter.

REFUGE DU PLA DE LA LAU
⌂

927m
2 buildings, each with room for 4 people, with partitions and provision for a fire.

0:10

Cross the footbridge over the Riberot stream and make your way to the right towards the Gardes footbridge.

Passerelle des Gardes

The forest road ends here at a parking area situated on the left bank of the stream. Leave the forest road, the 'chemin du Mont Vallier', and walk beside the torrent, climbing obliquely over a wooded slope and twisting through tight bends beside the cascading Muscadet stream. Cross the Aouen stream at roughly 1,250 metres and soon after, as you emerge from the forest, turn north and climb up a zigzag path on to grazing land.

1:50

CABANE DE LITOURNEAU
⌂

1,477m

0:30

Continue north, following the Aouen upstream, until you reach the Cabane d'Aouen.

CABANE D'AOUEN
⌂

1,620m.
Shelter for 5 people.

1:0

The route zigzags east along a stream, climbing up to a headland.

CAP DES LAUSES
⌂

1,892m
500 metres to the south-east, the Taus shelter provides space for 5 people.

0:40

Continue along the route, heading north-west for about 2 kilometres. First you walk along the flank of the Montgarie peak and then that of the Crabère peak before coming to the Laziès pass.

Col de la Laziès

1,840m.
Access to the Pays de
Bethmale.

1:30

COL D'AUÉDOLE
⌂

(see map ref D)
1,730m
Spring water down
below on the eastern
side

1:30

Etang de Bethmale

1,060m.
Junction with D17 which
connects Bordes-sur-Lez
(8km) to Seix (19km).
Large forester's house, not
open to the public; popular
beauty spot

1:30

Pas de la Core

(see map ref E)
1,395m
(12m)
An imposing pass at the
northern extremity of Valier
chain; situated between
basins of Salat and Lez;
crossed by D17, linking
Seix
to Bordes-sur-Lez (15km);

1:15

From here the GR10 turns east, passing to the south of a drinking trough and then climbing 100 metres to a little pass. It drops down to the pool of Ayes (1,694 metres) and climbs north-east towards the Auédole pass.

At this point, there is a junction with the alternative GR10, which leads to the marble quarries of Estours, via the Pas de la Core, where it again meets the GR10, and the Soularil pass.

Descend, heading north-east, from the col to the Eliet shelter. From here, continue north-north-west, down into the forest of Cadus, cutting across a forest road and ending up opposite a collection of barns dotted over the flank of Mont Noir. You now follow an old track eastwards that runs down below and parallel with the forest road. A little further on you join the road for about 200 metres, before leaving it on a sweeping bend to take a footpath on your left that leads down to the Bethmale pool.

Skirt the northern end of the pool walking along the road, passing in front of the forester's house, where there is a viewing point. Head for the fisherman's hut on the east bank. The route rises to 1,100 metres, meeting the footpath from Mont Noir, which goes round southern shore of the lake. Now you climb above the level of the D17 as you make your way to the Pas de la Core. You will now be passing into the Clot corrie. In order to avoid walking along a hazardous rocky path of avalanche debris, from the Balam ridge, follow the road for about 700 metres and then, at an altitude of 1,200 metres, leave it to climb a twisting path up to the Pas de la Core (see map ref E).

From the Core pass the GR10 descends due east along the valley bottom until it turns right on to a forest track. Follow this for a short distance before transferring to a broad path going left. When you reach the Tariolle hut, take the path to the right that leads across the meadows towards Artigues d'Esbints. Ash trees line the route. When they end, a well-made path takes you around a brow to the left. You pass a barn and a shepherd's hut. Cross the meadow, veering first south-east

also junction with the GR10, which runs south-west to Auédole pass via Pool of Bethmale (only possible in good weather); and south-east to Estours marble quarries via Soularil pass

ESBINTS
⌂
(see map ref F)
810m

then north-east. Then walk along a well-marked footpath which goes down into the valley beside the Esbints stream until you reach the hamlet of Esbints.

Alternative route GR10 from Col d'Auédole to Carrieres de Marbre d'Estours. You would be ill-advised to use this route in bad weather.

Col d'Auédole
(see map ref D)
1,730m

1:30

From the pass go east for 750 metres, as far as the gorge leading up to the head of the Eychelle pool; here you are flanked by the formidable walls of the Balam. The path takes you east down to the foot of Balam. When you reach an altitude of about 1,467 metres, you will find yourself on a beautiful glacial terrace on the edge of the corrie. Continue to climb gradually north-east along a natural footpath following the upper limit of the wooded area, then descend the grassy slopes towards the Core pass.

Pas de la Core

0:45

The GR10 runs south-east from the col, along a level path above the road from which it very soon diverges. About 600 metres further on you enter the Aube woods, descending along the edge of a valley and immediately climbing again into a beech wood and back to an altitude of 1,400 metres, which you maintain en route to the Luzurs shelter.

CABANE DE LUZURS
⌂
1,410m

1:0

If you are not using the shelter, bypass it to the west by following an upward-rising path. This takes you through the Marty steps (a very dangerous thoroughfare at the beginning of the season) to the Casabède hut, which is closed to hikers. After a gentle climb south-eastwards you reach the Soularil pass.

Col du Soularil
1,579m

1:30

From the pass you descend south-east along a footpath which passes over grazing land, at an altitude of 1,500 metres. After 1 kilometre you reach the Subera hut, which is also closed to hikers. Here you leave the path and follow the stream down its right bank, emerging from the forest at the Lameza hut, which is once again closed to hikers. The path lurches

down the steeply wooded slope and passes a spring at 1,210 metres altitude. Keeping to the right bank of the stream you come to the Arros barns.

Granges d'Arros
1,023m
Arros barns are situated on the opposite bank of the stream

1:0

Continue along to the right side of the Arros. However, a little further on you cross via a footbridge and follow a path on the left bank, descending a steep slope beside a conduit that supplies the hydro-electric plant at the confluence of the Arros and Estours streams. You cross the Estours on a footbridge, just before reaching the hydro-electric plant, and thus come to the marble quarries of Estours.

Carrières de Marbre d'Estours

1:45

From the Esbints gîte the GR10 continues east. When it reaches a fork, turn right along a broad path and walk as far as the Esbints stream. Cross via the footbridge, and climb to the left on a path which leads through a boxwood forest. Then turn right on to the road leading to Aunac. After 300 metres, veer left into the Peyrot camp, and then follow a path to the right that leads into the hamlet of Aunac (776 metres). Pass through the hamlet and take the path south-east down into the valley of Coume-Chaude, following the road and crossing the river at the Salat bridge.

Pont du Salat
550m
Detour, *30 mins.*
SEIX
⌂ ⛺ ✗ ⚓ 🚌
Take the road north.

0:15

Continue south to the Lauga watermill.

MOULIN LAUGA
⌂ ✗ 🚌
(see map ref G)
51m

1:0

Fork right to the west, cross the Salat again and then the Estours as it approaches Couflens-de-Betmajou. Climb south-west along a tarmac road leading into the Estours valley and then to the marble quarries.

Carrières de Marbre d'Estours
675m
The Arros and Estours streams meet at this point. A tarmac road leads to the watermill of Lauga; the route taken by the GR10 as it descends to Estours from Esbints and the Core pass.

1:15

Follow the river upstream to the Artigue hut.

Cabane de l'Artigue
(see map ref H)
1,053m
ONF hut closed to hikers.
View across corrie of
Artigue, with Mont Valier
towering in west and
Arcouzan waterfall.

1:40

CABANE D'AULA
⌂
1,550m
Shelter fitted out for 12
people, with fire and water
source.

1:40

Cabane d'Arreau
1,696m
Hut closed to hikers, but
you can shelter in sheep
pen.

1:0

Col de Pause
1,527m

1:45

COUFLENS
⌂ ✕ 🚋 🚌
(see map ref I)
702m
Tungsten mines, the best
in Europe; breathtaking
route to Port d'Aula along
untarred road

0:40

ROUZE
⌂
930m
Gite d'Ustou

1:20

Continue to climb up the valley to the head of the corrie and, at the top of the first waterfall, take the footbridge across the Artigue river. Now wind you way up into the wood of Pech d'Aula to a shelter.

Climb south-east then east, passing over a col at 2,000 metres. Next, cross over a grassy area and then scree to arrive at a forester's hut, which is closed to hikers, and the pool of Arreau. Descend to the shelter.

Strike out north-east dropping to an altitude of 1,620 metres where you meet a tarmac track, the D703. Stay on the track for about 700 metres and then leave it on your left to head west passing a small peak and ending up at the Col de Pause.

Leave the pass by walking along its eastern side on an ancient herdman's path. Cross the D703 several times, eventually rejoining it at the barns of Ribe du Prat, stay on it until you reach the Lasserre barns (1,100 metres). Continue from Lasserre to Faup, then to Faup à Raufaste and Casteras, where the path falls steeply at the base of the Quer mountain chain to pass through Angouls and then head east along the road to Couflens.

The GR10 leaves Couflens to the north, following the D3 to the little bridge over the Rouze stream. Keep to the right-hand side, crossing over at Maletague (880metres) as you approach the hamlet of Rouze.

The route passes the gateway to the gîte and then meanders up to Couret Maury, weaving left beyond the barns towards the hamlet of La Bourdasse (1,282 metres). Continue due east through the village, climbing over wet ground. Just as you pass two ruined barns, the path divides. Take the right-hand fork and after two sharp bends climb due east to the Serre de Cot pass.

Col de la Serre du Cot
1,546m

1:0

The path winds down to the east, penetrating 300 metres into a wood, and then descends around a hairpin bend to the Crabude barns.

Granges de Crapude

0:30

Follow the route above a stream for 150 metres. Cross a field with a stone boundary and leave the footpath to take a shortcut towards a group of barns, where you rejoin the path. Down to the left lies the hamlet of Bielle; you turn right, climbing gradually over a hill into Saint-Lizier.

SAINT-LIZIER D'USTOU
⌂ ♀ ⚓ ▭
740m
Gite at le Trein d'Ustou.

2:15

Leave Saint-Lizier via the D38 (south) crossing the Roman bridge of Oque (726 metres). Climb towards the Fitté peak on a path which runs along the edge of Fougas wood and is marked out by the barns of Pontaud, Lacoume and Plagnol. The path then ascends to the right making three or four hairpin bends then crossing the upper reaches of a broad channel to reach the Fitté peak.

Fitté peak and pass.
(see map ref J)
1,387m
Detour, *30 mins*
GUZET-NEIGE
⌂ ⛺ ✗

0:50

Follow the almost level path. The GR10 provides an access route to ski station; follow track, negotiable by car, for 2km from Escots pass.

The path climbs up along an easy ridge, passing to the west of the Picou de la Mire chain and its summit, then descends again to the Col d'Escots.

COL D'ESCOTS
⌂
1,618m
Detour, *45 mins*
GUZET-NEIGE
⌂ ✗ ✗
1,440m
Follow the track, suitable for vehicles.

1:30

The GR10 descends south-east from the hut next to the pass. It bypasses a rocky hummock (1,559 metres), climbs south-east into a pine forest and then passes through rhododendrons and heather. Cross a rocky area, pass by a ruined hut and then climb down through channels between the rocks to the Casièrens corrie. Leave the corrie in a north-north-east direction, walking first along its right flank and then along the rocky rim of a ravine, until you reach a shelf that overlooks the valley. Skirt the Fouillet waterfalls (1,300 metres). The path then suddenly comes out into a huge basin.

Jasse de Fouillet
1,170m,
Detour, *1 hr*
AULUS
🏠 🏕 🚉 🚌
750m
Leave GR to walk along a level footpath, descending north to right of Fouillet stream, as far as D8 (see map ref K)

1:0

Continue upstream until you come across a flat-topped outcrop of rock (1,175 metres). Follow the route north-east, climbing towards a wooded summit that appears quite detached from the rest of the chain. The path levels out as it approaches the south-west corner of the Souliou plateau (1,280 metres). Climb in a south-easterly direction into a wooded valley, skirt the edge of a clearing, and scale a steep slope to the Etang de Guzet.

Etang de Guzet
1,459 metres

1:0

The footpath skirts the eastern side of the pool to reach the high plateau of Gusalech, an area dotted with huts, now in disrepair (1,580 metres). Leave the plateau by walking first south-east, and then along the upper edge of a forest. Follow the trail along the flank of a steep slope, over several channels gouged by an avalanche. The path curves sharply over a granite slab, to reach the Ars footbridge.

Passerelle d'Ars
1,485 m

0:50

Cross the bridge. The path maintains an altitude of 1,500 metres and follows a tight curve east-north-east around a rocky shelf. The d'Ars waterfall cascades from the top of this. At the confluence of the feeder streams, the path drops steeply along on the rocky right bank. After a few tight bends you can soon enjoy a full view of this stunning triple waterfall which is one the most beautiful in the Pyrenees. With the melting of the snows the three converge into a single cascade of 110 metres. After a short passage across a forest above the ravine, you reach the bridge of Artigous.

Pont d'Artigous
1,060m

0:35

Do not cross the bridge. Instead, take the twisting path down to join a track. After 1 kilometre, veer to the right (east) and into the undergrowth. At first the path runs beside the Ars river and then it draws away taking you to the Mouline bridge.

Pont de la Mouline
(see map ref K)
785m
Aulus lies to the west

2:20

The GR10 continues along a path, used by vehicles, and then turns right (east) to join the path running north which links with the D8 road. Cross over the road and join a footpath opposite. Pass a collection of barns and then cross the Escale de Hille stream. Follow the Mérigne stream for about 100 metres before

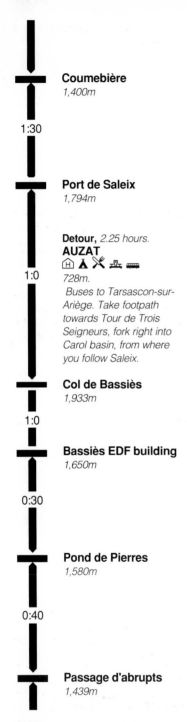

Coumebière
1,400m

1:30

Port de Saleix
1,794m

Detour, *2.25 hours.*
AUZAT

1:0
728m.
Buses to Tarsascon-sur-Ariège. Take footpath towards Tour de Trois Seigneurs, fork right into Carol basin, from where you follow Saleix.

Col de Bassiès
1,933m

1:0

Bassiès EDF building
1,650m

0:30

Pond de Pierres
1,580m

0:40

Passage d'abrupts
1,439m

crossing it. Then climb eastwards until you reach a dangerous precipice. Change direction and head for the Coumebière plateau.

Cross the road and continue south-east as far as the Lauze stream, which comes down from the Argentières peak. Note the old mineshafts. Carry on east for 500 metres, and then ascend via a number of extended hairpin bends along the left side of the lowest part of the valley to Port de Saleix.

Marked route north to Tour de Trois Seigneurs and Col de Port. Auzat (east) can be reached via a path along the Saleix stream.

From the Port de Saleix the GR10 climbs south, in the shadow of Mount Garias, to an altitude of 1,920 metres. From there it descends a steep slope to the Etang d'Alate, keeping to the eastern bank, and then ascending south-east to the Bassiès pass.

Descend south to the Plat de la Font (1,650 metres) and then veer south-east, skirting the successive lakes en route, to the EDF building near the dam on the largest lake.

The path continues to descend along the left bank of the stream, passing the Etang Long and making its way to the far end of the Etang d'Escalès. Here there is a small dam and a water supply point. (1,594 metres). The path ends here and you have to cross the stream via a stone bridge.

Once across the bridge, step away from the spillway and, a little further on, climb down a rock barrier. Return to a south-easterly course for 1 kilometre while you walk across a broad granite shelf. You stay at an altitude of roughly 1,450 metres. After a short ascent through a beech wood you come to a very steep incline.

An easily negotiated crossing. Once you have passed the *abrupts* (sleep slopes), descend a steep, stony path which takes you

0:30

down along the rim of the Bassiès ravine towards an aqueduct.

Old aqueduct
1,160m
This mountainside aqueduct unites the waters from the Marc and the Artigue above Auzat and the power station. However, it has been abandoned in favour of a tunnel.

1:0

Detour, *45 mins.*
AUZAT
⌂ ▲ ⚒ 🚌

Detour, see left. Cross the aqueduct and head for the hamlet of Hérout. From there follow path downstream, cross Vicdessos via cable car footbridge and follow road along stream.

The GR crosses the aqueduct and heads south, passing in front of a group of dilapidated huts. About half way down, cross a stream and use the path cut into the cliff, which brings you to a gallery.

Galerie
The gallery provides a conduit for the waters which rise on the eastern slopes of the Pla de l'Isard, away to the south.

0:20

After another 150 metres the path drops straight down to the hamlet of Marc and the D108, which you meet at a bridge.

Bridge and chapel of St. Antoine de Montcalm
Below the Maison Familiale and to the left of the bridge, take an old path which leads upstream to Mounicou. The route runs parallel to the road on the opposite bank.

0:20

MOUNICOU
⌂

(see map ref M)
1,087m
(2,199 metres)
Auzat or Vicdessos, the two main towns in the area, both lie at confluences of

After crossing the bridge at Mounicou, walk along the Andorra road for 130 metres before turning left on to a footpath known locally as the `Coumo de Bazerque' (an avalanche corridor directly above Mounicou). Keep to the right of the avalanche gully for five minutes then cross over and continue along the edge of the ravine, passing an EDF works platform

1:45

high valleys which run into Andorra and Spain over high passes, themselves at the feet of impressive massifs: Trois Seigneurs, Montcalm (3,080 metres), Bassiès (2,676 metres), Endron (2,472 metres) and Forcat (2,878 metre).

REFUGE DE PRUNADIÈRE
⌂
1,614m
(Water source)

1:45

Artiès
985m
Detour, 1hr
AUZAT
⌂ Å ⚍ ⚍
Follow road north.

1:0

Pradières Electricity Station
1,183m

1:30

ETANG D'IZOURT DAM
⌂
(see map ref N)
1,647m

1:0

Orris de la Caudière
1,942m

on your left. After two short bends you climb to the north-north-east, away from the ravine, only to return to it, for the last time, before ascending obliquely across the slope. Pass the Casteillous rock (1,500 metres) and, soon after, enter the forest, where you come to the Prunadière shelter.

From the forest house descend due north along a clearly marked path, skirting some very large rocks before climbing again, first north-east then north, to an altitude of 1,600 metres. Cross a wooded ridge and descend along the Prunadière passage, turning right (south-east) and following three hairpins bends into the sabouillet woods. The track from marc to Artiès heads off to the left, while the GR follows a zigzag path down the valley into Artiès.

Leave Artiès heading in a southerly direction along the road that leads to the Pradières electricity station. After 1.75 kilometres you reach a shortcut to Coumasses-Grandes.

Alternative route from GR10 to Coumasses-Grandes (unmarked). (2hrs). This steep climb enables you to cut across to Coumasses-Grandes (1,580 metres) and thereby avoid the Etang d'Izourt.

Continue along the road to Pradières.

Continue upstream, taking the lowest path, which draws close to the torrent and then, via a rocky gorge, scales the side of the escarpment. The path levels off and then climbs to the Orri de la Coume. It follows a cable up to the dam.

Alternative route GR10a from Etang d'Izourt dam to Refuge du Fourcat. Skirt the lake to the east and, at its southern end, climb the left bank of a stream. Zigzag your way up a steep slope, over a col to the Orris de la Caudière.

Cross the stream which flows from the Fourcat lake and climb south-west towards the cliffs.

The well-made path starts in the rocks about 150 metres from the stream, and rises up towards a ravine which it briefly overlooks. Then at 2,200 to 2,300 metres it climbs, parallel to the stream, up to an intermediate plateau. Note the beautiful waterfall. Finally it scales a rocky ridge and heads towards the Men of Stone (Hommes de Pierre).

1:30

Hommes de Pierre
2,350m
Huge cairns at the entrance to a corrie. The Fourcat is a fork-shaped corrie, set amongst the frontier peaks.

0:30

Now head down to the northern tip of the little Fourcat lake (2,339 metres) and climb upwards along its western bank. At the point where you come in sight of the larger lake (2,420 metres), turn east across the reef of fleecy-looking rocks to reach the Fourcat shelter.

REFUGE DU FOURCAT
⌂
2,445m

1:0

While the GR10a wends its way east along the Etang d'Izourt, the GR10 turns north, rising over the slopes and crossing several small waterways. The route passes above an EDF installation and then runs just below the Orri de Journasque. Descend gradually past a rocky shelf until you reach a point above the Coumasses-Grandes shelter.

COUMASSES-GRANDES
⌂
1,580m
Shortcut to join GR10 in valley. Shelter with room for 6 people.

1:0

Continue over steep rocky slopes overlooking the valley and then a wooded part where corridors alternate with steep slopes. As you approach the head of the valley, you come across a large rock. From here there is a view down to Artiès, A little further on you reach another viewing point, marked by a commemorative stele.

Stèle commemorative
(see map ref 0)
1,410m
Stone slab celebrating inauguration of Ariège section of GR10, 10 October 1975.

2:45

Alternative route GR10B from commemorative stele to Esquérus pass. Continue along a level path in the upper reaches of the Goulier valley beneath the Endon peak. Skirting the Pijol ridge, you come to the source of the Bosquets (1,413 metres). The path runs south-east over the avalanche-scoured slopes, across the Goulier stream and the Caudéras chain. Yopu pass above the Prade shelter (1,500 metres) (currently closed to walkers) and join the road leading down to Goulier. Leave it after 500 metres to link up with the path that runs north, parallel with the road. After about 1 kilometre veer to the right to rejoin the GR10 ascending from the Risoul pass. Continue north-eastwards to the Esquérus pass.

© IGN carte N°2148

Esquérus pass
1,467m

The GR10 descends north-east from the stele to the forest keeper's house (1,320 metres) situated above the Bertasque Road, which leads up beyond the Brosquet spring. Follow a broad path that crosses the road, thus cutting out a long hairpin bend, before rejoining the road and following it into Goulier.

GOULIER
⌂
1,110m

0:45

Detour, *1hr*
AUZAT
Ⓗ 𝗔 🚂 🚌
Take the Olbier-Capounta footpath.

Climb east, then north-east, from the village, along the Risoul miner's track, which is a popular tourist route leading to the Risoul pass.

Risoul pass
1,330m
Forest road leading

0:50 *to Grail pass.*

From the Risoul pass, the GR10 follows the Esplas ridge towards the Esquérus pass, meeting with alternative route, GR10B, at an altitude of about 1,400 metres. The two GRS follow the same route north-east to the Esquérus pass.

Esquérus pass
1,467m

0:45

A very picturesque footpath takes you south-east towards the head of the Sem valley, through a high section of forest on the edge of grazing land. Cut across the heads of the ravines and 1 kilometre further on you reach the Grail pass.

Grail pass
1,485m

0:30

At the left-hand corner of the forest keeper's house, begin to climb northwards. After about 10 minutes, you reach a fork, with a path leading off left down to Sem and the mines. Keep straight on towards the Lercoul pass. Note the fine view west over the Bassiès massifs of Montcalm and Endron.

Lercoul pass
1,549m
A broad grassy crossing between the peaks of Bède and Ganchette.

1:0

Continue north-east, down through a wood of box, beech and hazel trees. After a while, turn north towards a shoulder of the Saint-Tanoque mountain, where you will see a cross. Take the Lercoul Road for 300 metres in order to join an old track on your left that leads down to the village.

Lercoul
(see map ref P)
1,120m

In front of the church, take the Siguer Road out of the village and stay on it for 1 kilometre until, on the turn of a hairpin bend, you take a

0:50

An old mining village, with panoramic view over Siguer valley.

SIGUER
🏠 🍷 ⚓ 🚌
740m

0:45

Gestiès
960m

1:30

Col de Gamel
1,390m
Water source 400 metres south-east, along level path.

1:0

Bède ridge
1,642m

1:15

COL DU SASC
🏠
(or Séguer)
1,798m
Country road leading to Miglos via Larnat pass; water source to the west on path running alongside of Siguer (or Séguer) valley

2:20

shortcut, heading straight up towards the woods for 250 metres, and then left along an old track. Rejoin the road just before you reach Seuillac and the Siguer bridge.

From the centre of the village, an old track runs to the left towards Gestiès. It crosses the first loop of the road and, as it climbs north-east, touches the road again on successive bends.

Leave the village by passing to the right of the church and climbing east-north-east. A little further on, turn due east and head for the Gamel col.

The GR runs south-west from the pass towards a rocky outcrop on the edge of a ridge. Follow an almost level path due south along the mountainside, passing above the Labugé ravine on your way towards an outcrop, known locally as Egoumenou (1,455 metres). Here you leave the mountainside path, which carries on to the Sasc pass. Instead, climb eastwards over the rocky slopes to the Bède ridge.

Climb on to the ridge, reaching an altitude of 1,708 metres, and continue up to the Pla de Montcamp (1,904 metres) from where you will have fine views across to the mountain chain of Vicdessos and the Haute-Ariège. Now follow a clearly marked path that runs south over pasture land towards the Sasc pass.

From the Sasc pass you climb south for 500 metres up the grassy slopes (1,850 metres) and then the same distance again south-east as you pass above the sources of the Prade stream. You come to a ruined *orri* (hut) where you leave the Pas de l'Escalier path to descend east-south-east to Courtal Marti (1,812 metres) crossing a country road on the way. Head towards a group of large rocks on the edge of a plateau to the south. From here, veer to the right towards a small gully of the Balledreyt stream and descend eastwards to the Balledreyt shelter.

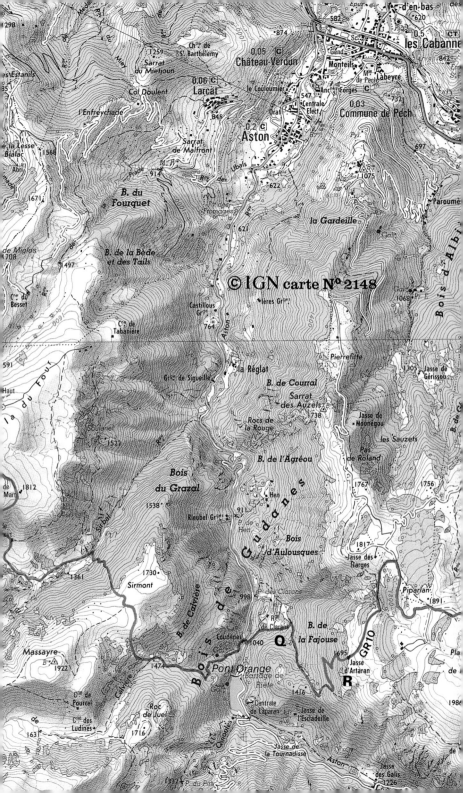

© IGN carte Nº 2148

BALLEDREYT SHELTER
⌂

*Room for 3 people
all year*

Descend to the left bank of the stream, follow it briefly before crossing it and heading towards the large rocks and woodland on the right-hand side of the Balledreyt valley. Continue along these rocks as far as the rocky rim of the main Sirbal valley. Now descend to the northeast, coming into a passage between the rocks that opens out into the Jasse de Sirbal (1,350 metres). Below the Jasse de Sirbal, cross the stream and head east southeast to enter a wood. The path makes a number of hairpins bends upwards, and then heads south to the Sirmont col.

Col de Sirmont
1,693m

2:0

Cross the col and, as you reach wet ground, gently descend southwards to join the path that leads into a little wood. Cross a stream and turn east-south-east through undergrowth. The path decends a very steep slope across rocks and bracken towards the area of Calvière (1,474 metres). Walk eastwards along the right-hand side of the stream, and wind your way through the undergrowth. Cross the Pont Orange in order to join the track that leads to Coudènes.

Coudènes
1,040m

Leave Coudènes by crossing over the bridge and, turning left, following the track for 300 metres. At the entrance to a little gorge, a path leads off north to the Clarans shelter.

Detour, *10 mins.*
CLARANS SHELTER
⌂

2:20

*(map ref Q)
10 people; fires possible; water*

The GR enters the gorge, crosses a stream and ascends to the edge of some pastureland. Join a twisting, rising path, skirt a little clearing, cross a stream, and follow the other bank up to a second clearing. From here you turn north-east on to a footpath that makes a number of sharp bends, runs through broomy woods and comes out on the grassy slopes of the Jasse d'Artaran.

Jasse d'Artaran
*(see map ref R)
1,695m*

1:35

From the hut you head north-north-east along a track which is quite suitable for vehicles. Cross a small valley and, about 500 metres further on, turn right on to another track, which initially leads due south at an altitude of roughly 1,800 metres. The track then turns east past the Piparlan hut (1,891 metres) and continues east towards the Beille d'en Haut shelter.

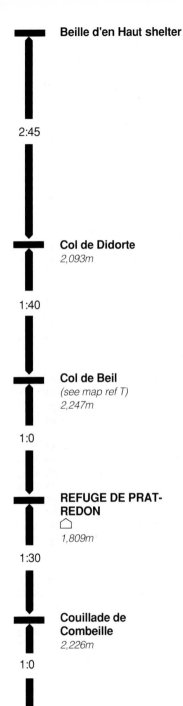

Beille d'en Haut shelter

2:45

Col de Didorte
2,093m

1:40

Col de Beil
(see map ref T)
2,247m

1:0

REFUGE DE PRAT-REDON
⌂
1,809m

1:30

Couillade de Combeille
2,226m

1:0

Continue south-south-east, walking along the side of a mound; at the end of the track climb along the top of the ridge to Prat Moll, its highest point. Keeping to the ridge-top, you pass two more mounds before descending, from an altitude of 1,983 metres, past a ruined hut to the Finestres col. From here the ridge climbs again, making its way towards two copses of pine trees situated on a rocky shelf; at which point you should follow the footpath that leads down to an area of little ponds. You can now see the Col de Didorte. Keep to the mountainside and remain at the same altitude. Cross over the scree to reach the Col de Didorte.

If you climb south-east up to the beginning of the ridge (2,278 metres), you will find markers for the `Tour des Montagnes d'Ax' which leads north-north-east towards Castelet and Ax-les-Thermes in the Ariège valley (see map ref S). At the start of the ridge the GR10 turns due south towards the Crête des Isards, a ridge orientated north-east/south-west. Follow this ridge south-west as far as the Beil pass

Leave the pass heading in an east-south-east direction, walking down the left side of a stream towards the Jasse de Lédranou. Cross the stream at an altitude of 1,800 metres and enter the Jasse de l'Orri Vieil, emerging 400 metres further on, once again on the other bank, and directly in front of the Prat-Redon shelter.

From here follow the valley, crossing the stream beneath the shelter and climbing south for a short distance near the waterfalls. Bear left over the slope, cross the stream, and continue climbing east towards the clearly defined indentation in the Sarrat de Llerbes, known as the Couillade de Combeille.

The GR now descends east-south-east to the ruined hut in the huge Llerbes basin, where it joins the path leading to the Tute de l'Ours. There is a spring 500 metres along the path. You skirt the Etang de Rébenty peak, which lies to the east, and 1 kilometre further north, on the ridges above the Saquet plateau and Tute de l'Ours, you reach the Couillade de Llerbès.

Couillade de Llerbès
2,305m
Boarding point for the
Saquet ski-lift
Detour,
SAQUET SKI
STATION
✗
2,030m
Cable car for Bonsacre
plateau (1,380 metres)
where there is a road to
Ax-les-Thermes (720
metres) 8 kilometres away.
Check times of cable car
and shuttle

0:50

AX-LES-THERMES
🏠 ⛺ 🚉 🚌

0:50

Col du Savis
1,904m

JASSE DU COURTAL
MANENT
⌂
1,600m
Water

0:30

Pont des Pierres
1,538m

0:45

MÉRENS-LES-VALS
🏠 ⌂ ✗ 🚉 🚌
▱
1,050m

From the Couillade de Llerbès, the GR10 descends along the ski run to a point just beyond a hummock (2,168 metres) and below the Etang Rébenty peak, where the Estagnols stream has its source. Follow the stream, first on its left bank and then, at roughly 2,000 metres, in front of a series of rock steps, you cross to the other side. Continue along the mountainside to the Savis pass.

Just down to the east, there is a good viewing point over the Ariège valley. From here you turn south-south-west down towards the Mourgouillou valley, crossing over the grassy slopes above the woods; and finally, turning south, you reach the Jasse du Courtal Manent.

Carry on to the south-western tip of this *jasse,* heading towards the Gadine stream. There you take the path down into the main Mougouillou valley, arriving at Planel des Llabérolles (1,550 metres), opposite the Fontaine des Fièvres. Here the GR abruptly changes direction, orientating itself north-east towards the Ariège valley as it follows the river downstream along its left bank. Cross over via the Pont des Pierres, 400 metres further on.

Descend along an old gravel track to a huge platform at the exit point of a gallery, where it joins an EDF road. About 100 metres beyond the second hairpin bend, leave the road and turn left on to the old path, bordering the Ubac woods, which leads into Mérens.

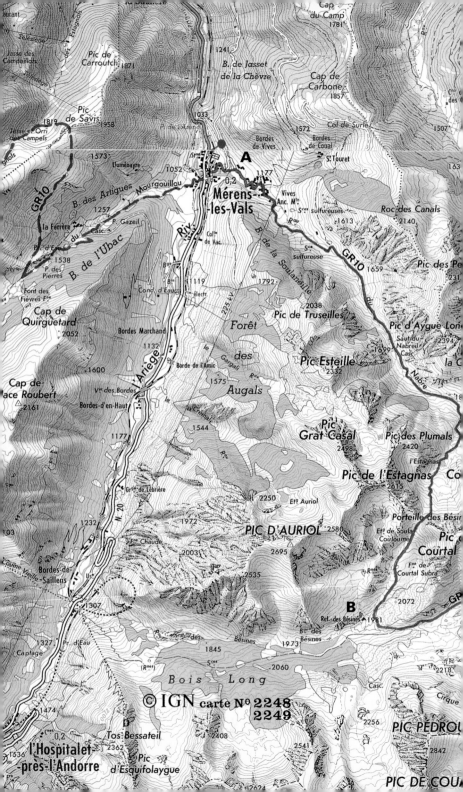

© IGN carte Nº 2248
2249

WALK 4

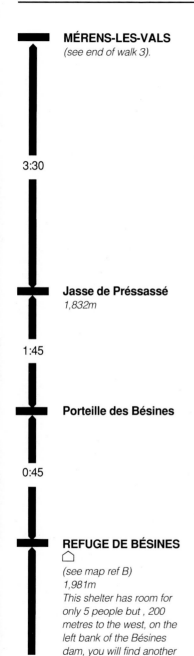

MÉRENS-LES-VALS
(see end of walk 3).

3:30

Jasse de Préssassé
1,832m

1:45

Porteille des Bésines

0:45

REFUGE DE BÉSINES
⌂
(see map ref B)
1,981m
This shelter has room for only 5 people but , 200 metres to the west, on the left bank of the Bésines dam, you will find another with room for 6.

1:40

Leave the N20 in the centre of the village, passing under the railway bridge and then over the River Nabre. Go past the church and, before you reach the gîte, climb up alongside the channel that regulates the flow of the Nabre. You link up with the road from Mérens-d'en-Haut in front of a burnt-out Romanesque church. Cut across the hairpin bend and follow the road until 100 metres beyond the bridge over the Redon stream, you come to a footpath on your left, which climbs south-east along the right bank of the Nabre. Pass a derelict barn, a spring and then a waterfall, the Saut de Nabreil. At roughly 1,750 metres you cross over to the left bank of the stream via a footbridge, and continue along this side as far as the Jasse de Préssassé.

The GR10 veers south towards the Estagnas ravine and returns to the left bank, bearing south-east then south-west in its passage across a sort of col (mountain pass) on its way to the little lake of Estagnas (2,056 metres). The path skirts the lake along its western edge and climbs south-south-west to Porteille des Bésines.

Leaving Porteille des Bésines, the path continues along the left bank of the stream and, following a south-westerly direction, runs down along fairly steep grassy banks into a rocky area strewn with large juniper trees and stunted pines. At an altitude of roughly 2,000 metres the GR10 crosses over to the right-hand bank of the stream and brings you to the Refuge de Bésines.

Continue down into the valley and follow the right bank of the main stream in an easterly direction. At an altitude of roughly 2,050 metres the GR splits away from the stream and, passing to the left of a little hill, it continues in a north-easterly direction along the right bank of a tributary. At the foot of a rock step, the footpath peters out. Cross over the water and, off to your right in an easterly direction, you pick your way up the scree of a gully that

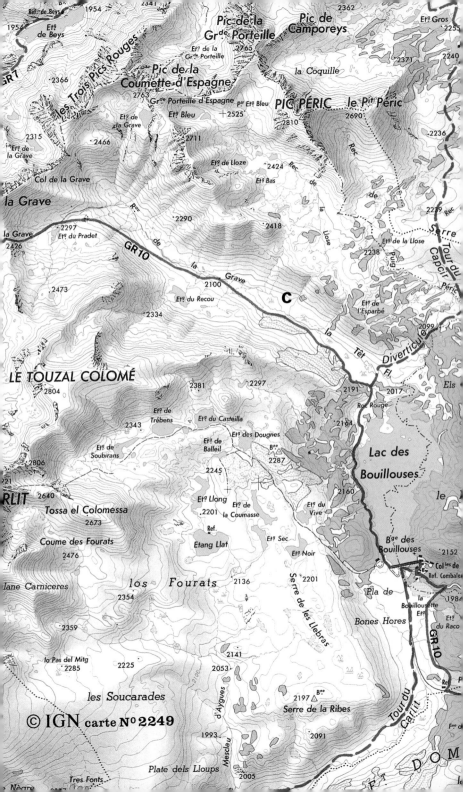

leads out on to the pastures of Bésineilles (2,350 metres), a grassy basin with a small lake lying in a gravel hollow. Clamber up the scree, eastwards, to the Col de Coume d'Agnel.

Col de Coume d'Agnel
2,470m

Descend east and then south-east; at an altitude of 2,390 metres you pass a broad grassy shelf to the right before the route slopes south-south-east down to the small lake of Lanouset, which is on the way to the northern tip of the Etang de Lanous (Lanous lake).

On the col de Coume d'Agnel you are standing on a major European watershed. To the west, the stream of the Bésines, which feeds the Ariège and then the Garonne flows into the Atlantic. To the east, the water from the Etang de Lanous, along with the Puymorens stream, accumulate via the rivers of Carol, Segre and Ebre until they flush into the Mediterranean.

1:15

Just before you reach a small hill, the GR10 meets the GR7 coming down from the Porteille d'Orlu and the shelter at En-Beys, in the north. They run together for a short distance before reaching a mound with a shepherd's hut situated above it, where they part company. The GR7 follows the east bank of the Lanous towards the La Guimbarde shelter, while the GR10 climbs due east up the grassy slopes to the wide pass named Porteille de la Grave.

Porteille de la Grave
2,426m

Leave the Porteille de la Grave by walking eastward along a winding path, which is sometimes covered by snow at the beginning of the season. You reach the small lake Pradet at its northern outlet. Keeping to the right bank and gradually veering south-east, continue down the path into the valley of the Grave. You will need to keep a wide berth between yourself and the boggy area alongside the river; the GR route markers follow one of many tracks that run parallel with it.

1:15

Pla Marécageux de la Têt
2,050m

The GR10 now turns south and climbs up through a narrow pass, providing a good view of the lake. Follow the west bank of the

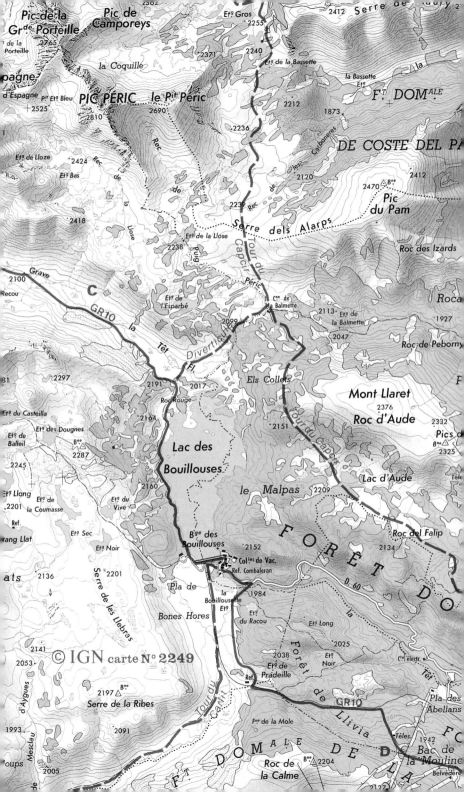

1:0

At this point the Grave stream turns into a river, the Têt, which flows through this marshland and eventually feeds the large Lac de Bouillouses, which is a conservation area. (See map ref C)

lake along a footpath, which is very popular with holidaymakers and leads to the Bouillouses dam.

BARRAGE DES BOUILLOUSES

⌂ ◠ ✗

The D60 is a popular road link with Mont-Louis (14km) and Font-Romeu (12km), where you can leave a car, or hitch a ride

1:45

Cross the wall of the dam to the opposite shore. From the Combaléran CAF shelter the path descends 500 metres to a footbridge over the Têt. Cross the river and follow the path along the edge of the forest. When you reach a point above the mountain pool of Pradeilles, turn south-west. Past a stone shelter and follow a track eastward into the forest. Keep on this track for 1 kilometres before turning right on to a footpath, which runs down to a stream. From here the path climbs across a ski run and broadens out as it runs along the mountainside in a south-easterly direction. Eventually, you pass a ski-lift pylon and reach the Pam pass.

Col de Pam
(see map ref D)
2,005m
A huge clearing with ski-lift and carpark

Detour, *1hr 30mins*
FONT-ROMEU
⌂ ✗ ▭ ▰
1,741m
From the Col de Pam, follow the S20 red route, which runs south-east alongside the ski-lift. It then turns south-westwards and finally south en route to the hermitage.

1:30

Detour, *1hr*
L'Ermitage
From there take the S8 red route westward for a short distance and then, turning left, (south) the S7 yellow route which takes you down to Font-Romeu

From the Col de Pam, the GR10 follows a ski-run along a ridge in the forest. Then, sweeping around to the right at green marker 27 it links up with a footpath on the left. Follow this beside a barbed-wire fence. Then descend to the right in a southerly direction, until you reach a crossroads on the N618 (1,730 metres).

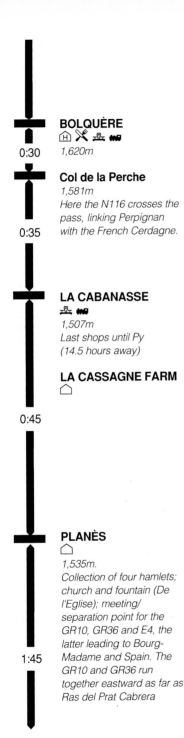

BOLQUÈRE
⌂ ✗ ⛬ ☷
0:30   *1,620m*

Col de la Perche
1,581m
Here the N116 crosses the
pass, linking Perpignan
with the French Cerdagne.
0:35

LA CABANASSE
⛬ ☷
1,507m
Last shops until Py
(14.5 hours away)

LA CASSAGNE FARM
⌂
0:45

PLANÈS
⌂
1,535m.
Collection of four hamlets;
church and fountain (De
l'Eglise); meeting/
separation point for the
GR10, GR36 and E4, the
latter leading to Bourg-
1:45   *Madame and Spain. The*
GR10 and GR36 run
together eastward as far as
Ras del Prat Cabrera

From here the route overlaps with the D10 through the forest and 1 kilometre further on, takes a shortcut, cutting across bends in the road as it makes its way into the village of Bolquère.

Follow the D10 out of the village for 1 kilometre passing the railway station, and coming to the pass of La Perche.

From the pass the GR10 follows the little road towards Eyne (D33) for about 100 metres until it turns off sharp left (east) along a track, which borders a plantation. This grassy track is an old Roman road that leads under the high tension cable in an east-north-easterly direction, finally joining the D32 just before it enters the village of La Cabanasse.

Alternative route to Planès via La Cassagne farm. Refer to the map for the waymarked alternative footpath and allow 45 mins to reach the gite, and the same again to rejoin the GR10 at Planès.

Take an eastern route out of the village and leaving the road to Mont-Louis on your left, follow the little road towards the hamlet of Moulin. About 100 metres beyond the outlying houses of the village, turn right (south) cutting across towards Planès. A little further on you will find a footpath on your left, that meanders south-east and then south. It crosses a stream, climbs east across a little valley, and then twists its way towards the D32. Follow this road to the outskirts of Planès.

Follow the route to Del Mig, the second hamlet. Just after the bridge over the river, take the lane up to the third hamlet, De l'Eglise (see map ref E).
If you visit the church, you should return to the fountain, and then make your way towards a sort of col; from there climb for 50 metres up a forest track before turning south-east on to a footpath which climbs through the forest to the Pla de Cédeilles. This is a sort of col or shelf on a spacious grassy crest.

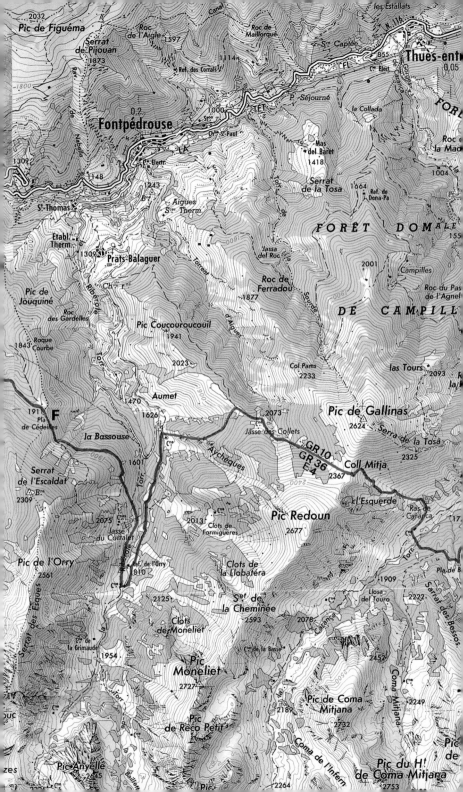

Pla de Cédeilles
(see map ref F)
1,911m
*Views over the Cerdagne
and Mont-Louis on one
side and, on the other, the
Valley of Prats Balaguer
and the foothills of
Carança.*

1:10

From the edge of the plain, head south along a level footpath into the woods. Cross a ravine with the stream below and then descend to the south-east, entering a forest and walking along a footpath which is overgrown by scrub and bushes. You walk towards the Ribérole stream and then follow it westwards, along the left bank. This takes you across spacious pasture land to an old shepherd's hut. Cross the river via the footbridge and walk down to the Refuge de l'Orry.

REFUGE DE L'ORRY
⌂
1,810m

PRATS BALAGUER
⌂
(4 people)

2:45

From the Refuge de l'Orry, follow the earth track, which runs down along the right bank of the stream, until you reach the path leading up to Prats Balaguer (see left). At this point, the GR breaks away from the path and heads south-east up a grassy slope strewn with broom and wild raspberries. Continue along a footpath which climbs a steep spur to an altitude of 1,895 metres where you will find a scout marker cross.

Pass through a storm battered forest and rejoin the trail at a bend, close to the Font dels Collets, climbing the twisting path until your reach the Coll Mitja.

Coll Mitja
2,367m
*Gracefully curving pass
with views over Cerdagne
and Carlit massif.*

1:0

At the pass, take a broken track downwards which brings you to a broad grassy shelf. Cross this, heading for the shelter on the river bank at Ras de la Carança.

ABRI DU RAS
DE LAS CARANÇA
⌂
1,831m

2:10

From the shelter, take a southerly route, crossing the river via a slatted wooden bridge. Follow the grassy track leading eastward until it starts to veer away to the left (east-south-east), at which point you climb up another grassy track to the right (due east). Continue to climb south-eastwards, passing a group of dilapidated huts. When you see a small plateau ahead of you (1,940 metres), veer away to the left (east-south-east) through the grass. Cross a stream via the bridge, or the ford, and then follow the grassy path north-east over a bushy, rocky patch of land to a marshy shelf. Here, you take a path which climbs eastward to the Jasse des Clots (1,910 metres), a broad grassy plateau. From the Jasse des Clots the GR10 continues eastwards. However, the route is not always clearly distinguishable. You pass a mound

(1,970 metres), and then the track leads east-south-east into a grassy gorge adorned with gentians, campanulas, broom and rhododendrons. At an altitude of about 2,100 metres, the GR sweeps sharply eastward, around to the left, climbing steeply east then north-east along the right bank of a little valley, on a clearly marked path through the forest. It twists its way up the side of a rocky spur towards the north-east, reaching the meadowland beneath the Col del Pal, which is a broad grassy crest on the Serre Gallinière.

Col del Pal
2,294m

1:50

The path follows the contour line of the little valley of Caret in a south-east direction, first over open ground and then, after the ravine, across the upper reaches of a small wood and finally out into open territory. Note the marker stones. Also, you will find a large cairn on the Serre de Caret. Continue walking south-east along a clearly defined pathway which twists down a green, bushy slope and joins the track that leads from Mantet to Porteille de Mantet, which is on the frontier ridge. Descend north-eastwards along the left bank of a stream and cross it at about 1,500 metres altitude. Follow the path down until you come to Mantet.

MANTET
(see map ref G)
1,550m
Pretty village; well maintained 11th century church. Cemetery has a handsome iron cross dating from 1573. Village is currently engaged in a spirited debate over whether or not to establish a gîte for hikers.

2:15

Leave Mantet along an old road, in very poor repair, which meanders north-east across meadowland as far as the Mantet pass, at which point you meet the road that links Mantet to Py. Take a shortcut down a zigzag path into the forest. When you rejoin the road keep on it for a short distance until you reach an old road which runs below the road you are on. Take this, twice cutting across the other road until finally you rejoin it to enter Py.

PY
1,023m

1:30

Leave the village by the lane that descends east below the fountain. Take the first road to the right and, beyond the public tip, cross over the River Rotja. Turn left (north) and walk along the right bank towards the hamlet of Farga. After passing the landing stage of a disused mine, take the grass path on your right which runs up through the woods to a

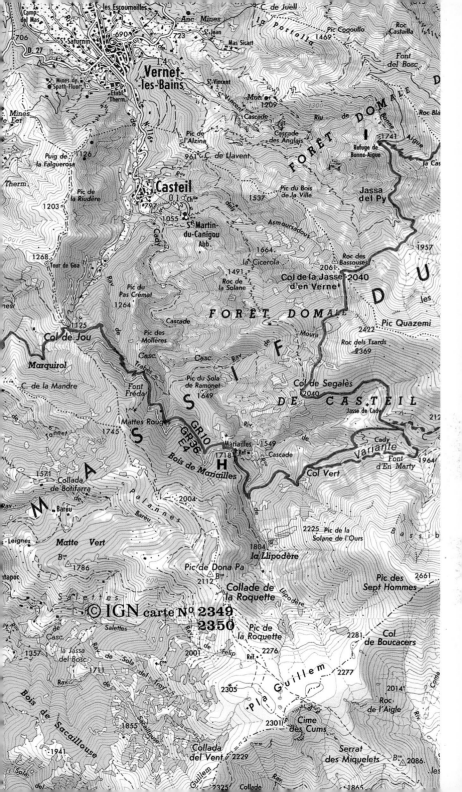

© IGN carte N° 2349
2350

pass (1,064 metres). The path descends and then climbs up to the Col de Jou.

Col de Jou

1,125 metres.
You are now entering the Canigou massif. The broad panorama offers views north-north-east across to the Tour de Goa. From here a path runs along the ridge to the Pena peak and then descends to Vernet-les-Bains. To the west, you will see the summit of Tres Esteles with its desolate slopes; and to the south-west the frontier chain and the peak of La Dona.

2:0

The track from the Col de Jou leads through the forest to Mariailles. Initially the GR follows this track, but then breaks away along an old track which climbs gradually eastward into the forest to the Créu pass, where it swings south and rejoins the forest track to Mariailles. Stay on this road for a mere 25 metres, leaving it on a hairpin bend, near a wayside table and bench, to strike due south along a footpath which climbs quite steeply into the forest. Pass the spring of Font-Fréda, wind your way up over the ridge (1,454 metres) and follow the path which runs parallel with the road as far as Mariailles.

MARIAILLES

⌂
(see map ref M)
1,718m

Detour, *30 mins.*
CASTEIL
🏠 ✕

Detour, see left. From the Col de Jou, it is 5 kilometres to Casteil, if you take the road. Alternatively follow the red path, marked INT no.1 on a gateway at the Col de Jou (close the gate behind you to protect the livestock). From Casteil follow the D116 for 2 kilometres to Vernet-les-Bains.

VERNET-LES-BAINS
🏠 ⌂ ✕ 🚠 🚌

2:15

From the pastoral shelter of Mariailles, take a southerly route down across a stream and then up towards the east into the forest. Cross over the Sept Hommes ravine and climb north-east to the Col Vert. From here take a path on your left and descend to the Cady stream, which you cross on stepping stones. Another leads off to the right towards the Pic de Canigou, but you follow the GR10 to the left (north-west) along an almost level path which crosses over loose rock and then through sparse woodland until it reaches the south-west ridge of the Quazemi peak at the Segalès pass.

Col de Segalès
2,040m

Bypassing the track on your left which leads down to Saint-Martin-du-Canigou, follow a path heading north-east. This rises gradually and then levels out at about 2,100 metres as

2 : 0

it slides over the Jasse-d'en Vernet pass. The path is well marked as it descends into the woods to the north-east, but then becomes obscured by tall grass as it leads towards Les Conques (1,880 metres), a region scarred by avalanches. The path now climbs east, skirting this wild countryside. Then it plunges into the woods then passes through an area of tall grass as it approaches the ravine of the Roc dels Izards. Cross this and follow the path as it twists on its way to the Jasse del Py. From here take the forest track to the shelter of Bonne-Aigue.

REFUGE DE BONNE-AIGUE
⌂
(see map ref I)
1,741m
The nearby spring is often dry in summer

From the shelter at Bonne-Aigue continue along the track for another 50 metres before turning south-east, to the right, along another path which meanders its way up into the forest. Cut diagonally across a clearing, named Jasse de la Casteille, where you will find a little drystone hut. Then continue north-eastwards, gently walking up into thinly wooded countryside. Cross the north-west ridge of the Joffre peak and climb towards the south-east. At an altitude of 2,250 metres, walk along the north-east spur of the Joffre, close to the regulated spring of La Perdrix. Soon after you come across the path that links the shelter at Les Cortalets with the Pic du Cinigou. This track is normally only in use during the summer months. Continue south-east along the path, then north-east, skirting a shallow lake. From here there is a classic view of the Canigou peak. Continue towards the chalet-hotel at les Cortalets.

2 : 0

CHALET-HOTEL DES CORTALETS
ⓗ ⌂
2,150m.
Set aside a whole day to explore the Canigou region; to ascend Canigou peak, 1hr 30 mins take the path from Perdrix well spectacular panoramic views in good weather.

The GR10 now follows a path marked `Balcon du Canigou'. However, there is an alternative route (see broken line on map). Behind the chalet at Les Cortalets (east), take the shortcut which meanders downwards to link up with the tourist road at Ras del Cortalets. Follow this road as far as Ras de Prat Cabrera.

1 : 0

Ras de Prat Cabrera
1,739m.
The GR34-E4 splits off towards Vinça and

Leave the road, which runs north down into the Llech valley. Instead, take a path heading south-west into open country. Cross the Lentilla river and then its tributary and proceed east

Mazamet.

2: 30

Col de la Cirère
(see map ref K)
1,731m

0: 30

Mines de fer de Batère
1,500m

1: 15

**Des Vigourats
intermediary station**
884m

through open country towards a forest. Pass the ruined shelter of Pinatell (1,650 metres) and meander into the forest to the maison de l'Estangnole at 1,479 metres (see map ref J).

The path climbs to the south into the forest and is easily distinguished, despite being narrow and steep in parts. It bends to the left (south-east) at the edge of the wood and begins to level out as it approaches the Cirère pass.

From here, head south-east, passing on your left first a cave and then deep mineworks. At an altitude of about 1,650 metres, the path slants off to the left (east) towards an old mineworking and then descends to the road that leads to the iron ore mines of Batère.

From the former canteen building, make your way down the road for 800 metres until you reach the Col de la Descarga (1,393 metres). There you leave the road and drop down to the north-east into pasture land to pick up the path which follows the right bank of a stream. After a while, the path swerves to the right and runs along the ridge of a spur. The path is quite visible as it descends, despite the undergrowth. At 1,090 metres you pass first a pylon and then a cable anchorage situated on a hillock which you skirt to the right as you descend south. From now on the route to Arles-sur-Tech roughly follows the ironworks cable. The `cable track' is by no means a continuous path: it breaks away to follow both old and new paths. However, it is bushy and shaded, which is very welcome during the summer. On reaching the Pla del Castella the path veers left (north) passing under the cable and then back again. Finally, it follows the cable as far as the Vigourats cable station.

Pass to the left of the station and then take a path to the left which twists down over a stream. Then climb east through the undergrowth, keeping close to the line of the cable. On a brow of a hill, above the path, lies the farm of Abadies (836 metres).

The GR passes south of the Abadies farm, crosses a track and continues east to a rivulet. Follow its right bank for 60 metres before crossing and threading your way along the other side. Join the path leading south-

1 : 0

**Jacouty intermediary
station**
620m

1 : 0

ARLES-SUR-TECH
(see map ref L)
282m

2 : 0

Col de Paracolls
902m

east from the farm, pass under the high voltage cable and then, following the track to the right, you arrive at the anchorage point at El Rey camp. Walk under the cable and take a path leading down to a recently made earth track. Turn right on to this and walk towards Jacouty.

Skirt the station to the left and return to the cable. Descend south-east along a footpath that follows a spur before plunging into a chestnut grove. You come to an earth road which you walk along as far as the last cable anchorage. Now take the footpath on your right which leads into the upper reaches of Arles, close to the campsite.

Continue downwards along the path, passing to the right of the mine pithead and crossing the River Tech via a footbridge. Pass a transformer situated near an irrigation canal and follow the concrete road for a short distance, before turning right onto a footpath which ascends south-east across terraced ground. The path forks left at an electricity post and, 50 metres further on, crosses a stream. Pass under a second electricity cable and climb up into the forest until you meet the road from Can Balent. Here you take a shortcut and, 250 metres before the farm, turn left. When you reach a fork, turn right and climb a twisting path in a south-south-east direction. Continue past Font de los Amors and on to the Paracolls pass.

From the pass, take a path which descends to the south through a chestnut grove. The path then ascends slightly to cross a spur and then continues along its flank. Cross a stream and then turn left (north-east) towards the derelict buildings of Paracolls. From there, walk in a south-south-east direction across level ground to a footpath which, beyond a sunken valley, runs east along a ridge and then twists downward. You pass a ruin, cross over a meadow and reach the En Souler ravine. Can Souler farm is on your right. This is private property, so walk a little downstream from the house where you can ford the river, paying particular attention to your footing when the river is in full spate. The route meanders up to a little road. Follow this for

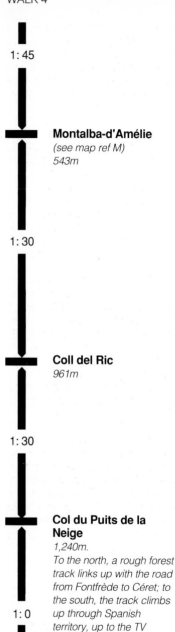

1:45

400 metres north-east, before breaking away to the left along a footpath that first climbs a spur and then winds down to the south-east of another spur. You can see the hamlet of Montalba off to your left. Cross the Coume ravine and turn left to follow its right bank as far as Montalba-d'Amélie.

Montalba-d'Amélie
(see map ref M)
543m

Follow the road to Amélie-les-Bains. On a sharp bend, just past the second bridge, break away from the road to pick up a path which cuts across the hairpin bends of the access road to Can Félix. Can Félix is private property, so make sure that you follow the route markers carefully in order to avoid trespassing. From here you link up with the old track that joins Amélie-les-Bains to the frontier at Roc de France. Cross the ravine of Salt d'Aigua and climb up to a chestnut grove which borders an enclosed tract of land. It is unwise to stop in this area. Continue along a path which climbs upwards, passing a sheepfold on the right, and reaching the top of the Ric pass.

1:30

Coll del Ric
961m

From the col, you tackle the steep gradient of La Pourasse, following the line of the ridge. A little further on, the path veers off left to join the ridge linking the Puig de La Pourasse with the Roc de France and continues to a junction of paths. Just before the frontier ridge it turns left (southeast then east) along an almost level path into the wood of La Marquise. You reach the Col du Puits de la Neige on the frontier ridge via the northern slopes of the Roc de Frausa.

1:30

Col du Puits de la Neige
1,240m.
To the north, a rough forest track links up with the road from Fontfrède to Céret; to the south, the track climbs up through Spanish territory, up to the TV transmitter at Ras Mouchet; to the south-east, you can see the shelter of Les Salines next to the hermitage.

From the pass you take a footpath that descends north-east across scree and then winds through the woods of La Comtesse. It passes beneath the grotto of Les Trabucayres and, having crossed over a little ravine, reaches the source of the stream. The path continues to drop. Pass the fork to the Soubiranne farmhouse on the left and continue to the right until you reach the Cirères pass

1:0

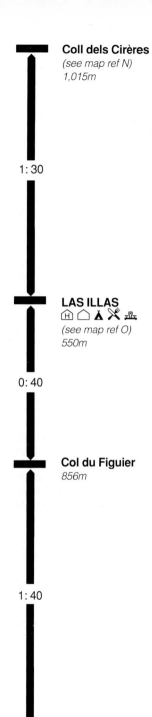

Coll dels Cirères
(see map ref N)
1,015m

1 : 30

LAS ILLAS
(see map ref O)
550m

0 : 40

Col du Figuier
856m

1 : 40

Leave the pass via a footpath along the Salines ridge, walking south-east for 150 metres before turning left along an almost level path. You reach a spur. On your left, there are the markings for an alternative GR10 route heading towards La Selve. Continue due south along a narrow path which winds across a patch of heather and broom. Cross a stream and descend along a ridge towards Llanson. At an altitude of 840 metres, leave the ridge and turn right (south) on to a path which leads to the head of a ravine. Here you follow a path for 30 metres before switching to a path on your right which crosses the ravine. Follow the GR route markers closely. At an altitude of 580 metres, the path fords the Salina River and, following the right bank, gradually slopes down to Las Illas.

Between Las Illas and Banyuls the route passes through very prickly vegetation, and you would be wise to stick to clearly marked paths, rather than follow alternative routes marked on your map. Take the Maureillas Road out of Las Illas, leaving the D13F on your left. After the bridge, continue for 100 metres before turning right up the lane leading to Super las Illas. Climb the concrete steps up on to a road and follow the signs to the Figuier pass.

From the pass the road continues south-east. However, the GR heads north-east along the track to Perthus, keeping on the French side of the frontier and occasionally coming very close to the ridge itself. The road can be furrowed and muddy after heavy rain and the vegetation tends to be prickly. It is important to follow this track carefully to avoid going astray on one of the many paths which cut across it. After 2 kilometres you pass to the right of the Nou farmhouse, then 600 metres further on, as you approach the Col de Porteille, there is a path on the left which leads down to Riunoguès. Continue to the right (south-east) approaching the frontier ridge and then follow its course north-east. The path switches sharply to the left around a hairpin bend, passes another fork to Riunoguès and continues roughly north-east towards the Col del Priorat.

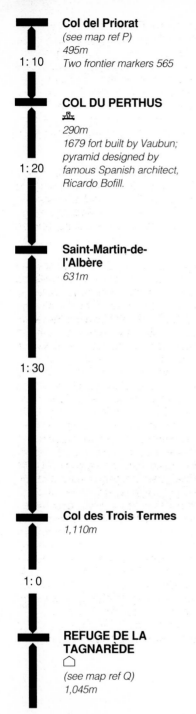

Col del Priorat
(see map ref P)
495m

1:10   *Two frontier markers 565*

COL DU PERTHUS
290m
1679 fort built by Vaubun;
pyramid designed by
1:20   *famous Spanish architect,*
Ricardo Bofill.

Saint-Martin-de-l'Albère
631m

1:30

Col des Trois Termes
1,110m

1:0

REFUGE DE LA TAGNARÈDE
(see map ref Q)
1,045m

Continue down the track for about 850 metres, then take a shortcut across a hairpin bend which brings you to the Mas Barder. After 200 metres you join a tarmac road which takes you to the Perthus pass.

Just before the car park on the French side of the frontier, leave the main road to join a minor road which climbs east towards Saint-Martin and the Col de l'Ouillat. Stay on this road for 4.5 kilometres. Pass under an aqueduct, by the Mas Reste farmhouse. After 50 metres turn right on to a track, then shortly after take a path to the left which leads to Mas Serre and thence eastward down a narrow street to the hamlet of Saint-Martin.

Leave the hamlet to your right, following the road heading northwards. Just before it joins the road to Néoulous, turn right on to a furrowed track, which is in fact the dry bed of a stream. Cross over a meadow and then through a wood of holm oaks. Cut across the road and then, a few minutes later, cross it again at the Col del Rat, a natural shelf on the south-west ridge of the Roc des Trois Termes. The route climbs north-east across a firebreak. The track is not always clear, but, you can just follow the edge of the spur. Skirt to the left of the Roque Courbe, and pass into a wood, carefully noting the markers. At about 1,000 metres, the path veers to the left, passing the spring of Euga Morte, on its way to the north-west ridge of Trois Termes. From there, walk south-east along a level path until you join the road at the Trois Termes pass.

Follow the road to the summit of Néoulous and walk to the left around the enclosure of the TV transmitter. Now descend due south-east to the Tagnarède spring. Fill up with water! Continue south-east towards the shelter of La Tagnarède, which is sandwiched between the frontier ridge on your right and a forest road to your left.

From the shelter, the path runs south-east through the forest, passing between the Pic Pragun to your right and the forest road lower down to your left. On the Pragun pass, the footpath disappears and you must watch out for the markers. Following these will ensure that you remain in French territory as you skirt the northern face of Puig del Talayadou. When you reach the Col del Faig with its frontier cross 584, head south-east over the grass, staying clear of the hill on your right. At the Col de l'Orry (974 metres) climb due east above a plantation on the French flank. Bypass the Puig de la Basses and Raz de la Menthe on your right, both outcrops of the main frontier chain.

Col de l'Estaque
1,023m

Keep the forest on your left and follow the path as it climbs north-east along the ridge to the Pradets peak. After a gradual descent to the Col des Emigrants, you climb again, due east, to the summit of the Quatre Termes peak.

Pic des Quatre Termes
(see map ref R)
1,156m

From the peak of the Quatre Termes the GR10 descends south-east and, at an altitude of 1,020 metres, the alternative route via Coulourmates branches off to the left. The path runs just to the left of the frontier ridge, in between the Massane col on your right and the Massane source on your left. Continue east on the French side, keeping above the treeline. Leave the Col and the Pic de la Carbassère, with its stone turret, well to the right, and continue north-east until you reach the Col del Pal (899 metres). From there climb steeply to the Pic de Sailfort (981 metres). Carefully pick your way east through the bushes and rocks, down along the ridge. When you come to a small, grassy col (561 metres), walk past it for a few metres and turn on to a path leading east. After about 2 kilometres, leave the path and once again follow the ridge to the Col de Baillaury (418 metres). From there climb north-east along a fairly steep path up to the Col de Fourmigou (488 metres) which lies beneath and to the south-west of the Tour de Madeloc. Follow the path which runs east along the southern flank of the Madeloc. The undergrowth is so bushy that you are forced to walk along the drystone wall. You pass the Reigt `cave' (470 metres), now in ruins, and head for the Gascons pass.

1:10

0:50

3:20

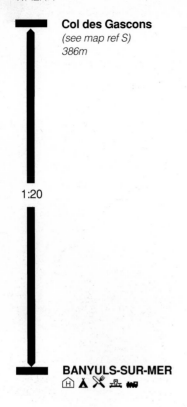

Col des Gascons
(see map ref S)
386m

1:20

BANYULS-SUR-MER

From the pass, you follow a road leading east for 60 metres before taking a shortcut to your left, which cuts across the hairpin bend and rejoins the road above the Chasseurs spring (280 metres), where you can quench your thirst. Stay on the road as far as the Llangastéra pass (256 metres), where you take the track that climbs up north-east towards the Puig Girand and then descends to Banyuls. You come to a fork where you turn right and pass alongside a renovated farmhouse called Corral Nou, keeping a little to the right of the edge of a spur, before following the track through a cork-oak wood. On a hairpin bend take a path leading straight ahead, along the edge of a spur, through a scorched forest. You descend across a vineyard, following an old track now overgrown with brambles. Cross a road and join a track leading into Banyuls. Take the fork to your right running south for 100 metres and then south-east along a little ridge above the sports ground. Pass a house and then cross under the railway line along a track which takes you to the Avenue Puig del Mas. Turn left and follow it into Banyuls.

INDEX

The many different kinds of accommodation in France are explained in the introduction. Here we include a selection of hotels and other addresses, which is by no means exhaustive — the hotels listed are usually in the one-star of two-star categories. We have given full postal addresses so bookings can be made.

There has been an explosive growth in bed and breakfast facilities (chambres d'hôte) in the past few years, and staying in these private homes can be especially interesting and rewarding.   Local shops and the town hall *(mairie)* can usually direct you to one.

Details of bus/train connections have been provided wherever it was possible. We suggest you refer also to the map inside the front cover.